How to Catch a Turtle

An Introduction to Mindfulness

David Franklin

How to Catch a Turtle

Copyright © 2025 by David Franklin

For information, contact:
David Franklin
@authordavidfranklin
https://davidsfranklin.com/

ISBN: 979-8-9922683-8-6
Library of Congress Control Number: 2025904994

Character design by Tyler Spence
Printed in the United States of America

First Edition

10 9 8 7 6 5 4 3 2 1

Dedication

To my mom... your faith, patience, and perseverance continue to inspire me. You taught me how to serve others, and for that, I am forever grateful.

And to those seeking stillness in a world that never slows down, may this book help you discover the peace that comes from being present. Mindfulness is not about the chase but about noticing what has always been within reach and inside of you.

"Nor will people say, 'Here it is,' or 'There it is,' because the kingdom of God is in your midst." (Luke 17:21 NIV)

A portion of the proceeds from each book will be donated to the following organizations:

Miles 4 Matthew (www.miles4matthew.org/) provides financial aid to families navigating the challenges of pediatric cancer.

Transformation Life Center (transformationlifecenter.org/) inspires the love of reading through the love of running to help black and brown boys improve reading proficiency, outrun childhood obesity, and live fuller, healthier lives.

Acknowledgements

I want to express my deepest gratitude to all those who have been part of my journey throughout life. Every experience, both the challenges and the support, has contributed to my growth and transformation, and for that, I am deeply grateful.

To those closest to me... thank you for the wisdom and clarity you've shared over the years. This book would not have been possible without these experiences with you all. Each of you has touched me personally and uniquely. In the meditative words of Ho'oponopono: "I'm sorry, please forgive me, I love you, thank you."

Lastly, the readers... thank you for choosing to embark on this journey of mindfulness and reflection. May this book offer you the peace and stillness you seek.

About the Author

David S. Franklin is a Navy veteran, ordained minister, mindfulness coach, and spiritual seeker whose life journey has been defined by service, personal growth, and a deep connection to the present moment.

With a passion for helping others discover the power of mindfulness, David's work focuses on guiding people toward greater awareness and inner peace.

David has studied under renowned mindfulness and spiritual teachers, including Rick Hanson, Jack Kornfield, Tara Brach, and Eckhart Tolle. His formal education spans Biblical Studies at Moody Bible Institute, Organizational Leadership at Penn State, and Machine Learning at MIT. He also completed the Global Health Care Leader program at Harvard Medical School, integrating both his spiritual and academic backgrounds into his holistic approach to personal transformation.

In *How to Catch a Turtle,* David shares reflections from his personal journey, offering a gentle guide to mindfulness and finding stillness in a fast-moving world. Beyond writing, he enjoys yoga, hiking, trout fishing, and collecting vinyl records. He is also in the process of writing *The Presence of Absence,* further exploring themes of awareness and spiritual growth. David views life as a continual process of learning, healing, and reconnecting with the present moment.

For more about David's journey and insights, visit *https://davidsfranklin.com/.*

Preface

The overarching preface of the storyline in the provided chapters centers around the practice and benefits of mindfulness, which is presented as a way to enhance one's mental and physical well-being by focusing on the present moment with openness and curiosity. This theme is explored through various aspects, including the origins of mindfulness, how to practice it, its benefits, and how it can be integrated into daily life and relationships.

It sets the stage by introducing mindfulness as a powerful tool for managing stress, improving emotional regulation, and enhancing overall well-being. It emphasizes that mindfulness is accessible to everyone and can be practiced in both formal meditation sessions and everyday activities. The storyline aims to guide the reader through understanding and incorporating mindfulness into their life, providing practical tips and insights along the way.

Here, the old fable of the rabbit and the turtle (Aesop's Fables: tortoise and the hare) can be seen as a metaphor for the principles of mindfulness described in the chapters:

The Rabbit: The rabbit represents a mind that is constantly rushing, multitasking, and seeking quick results. This can lead to stress, burnout, and missed opportunities for genuine connection and awareness.

The Turtle: The turtle embodies the mindful approach—moving slowly, steadily, and with purpose. By taking its time and being present in each moment, the turtle ultimately wins the race.

Just like the turtle, the practice of mindfulness encourages slowing down and paying attention to the present moment. It highlights the benefits of a steady, deliberate approach to life rather than rushing through it like the rabbit.

By exploring the roots of mindfulness in ancient traditions and its adaptation to modern practices, the chapters draw a parallel to the timeless wisdom of the turtle's approach—rooted in patience and consistency.

These sections underscore the advantages of adopting a turtle-like pace. By practicing mindfulness, individuals can achieve a sense of calm and clarity, reducing stress and improving mental health, much like the turtle's measured progress leads to victory.

Practical advice on beginning and maintaining a mindfulness practice aligns with the turtle's slow and steady progress. It emphasizes small, consistent efforts over time, contrasting with the rabbit's hurried and sporadic efforts.

These chapters illustrate how mindfulness can enhance interpersonal connections and manage stress, akin to how the turtle's steady pace and awareness lead to a successful outcome. Mindful interactions and stress management require patience and presence, mirroring the turtle's qualities.

Overall, the storyline uses the fable of the rabbit and the turtle as a powerful analogy to convey the essence of mindfulness. It encourages readers to adopt the turtle's approach in their own lives, promoting steady, mindful progress over rushed, impulsive actions. By doing so, they can achieve greater well-being, improved relationships, and a more balanced life.

"Most people are never fully present in the now, because unconsciously they believe that the next moment must be more important than this one. But then you miss your whole life, which is never not now. And that's a revelation for some people: to realize that your life is only ever now."

-Eckhart Tolle

Contents

Chapter 1: From Turmoil to Tranquility

"Mindfulness gives you time. Time gives you choices. Choices, skillfully made, lead to freedom."

-Bhante Henepola Gunaratna

The fable of the turtle and the rabbit competing in a race is known to every other person out there. The rabbit got overconfident in his ability to outrun the turtle and stopped to take a nap. But the turtle resolutely carried on, reaching the finish line before the rabbit and beating him at the race.

Unlike the rabbit, the turtle was mindful of his strengths and weaknesses as well as the scenario he was in. Being aware of the value of each minute, which amounted to his slow but steady success, made him continue walking while the rabbit took a nap. This fable shows that despite the heavy disadvantage the turtle had over the rabbit for walking slowly, he managed to turn the tables in his favor by staying consistent.

Similarly, life is a race for us, too, in which we have to maintain balance, no matter how against the odds are to our victory. And if we follow the example of the shrewd turtle, being mindful of our surroundings and ourselves, we can surely make it through the race.

But how can we be mindful? In our lives, as everything is already going too fast for us to control and so many different tasks occupy us at the same time, how can we be aware of our surroundings to the extent that we can be considered mindful?

The trick is to start with things that matter, and I have experienced firsthand how being mindful changed my life for the better. This book will guide you through my personal experiences and life on embracing mindfulness and why it is so important to live a mindful life.

Embracing Mindfulness and Meditation for Inner Peace and Love

At its core, mindfulness is staying in the present and balancing the thin line between past events and future realities. Being mindful is being aware of your surroundings, yourself, and everything connected to you. One of the common and effective ways to achieve this state of self-awareness is through meditation.

Through breathing exercises, chanting, or visualization, we can centralize the focus of our thoughts. This process is called *meditation* and is a common practice for connecting with one's self. Meditation helps us learn to be a watcher of our thoughts, an observer who connects with those thoughts and interprets them according to his self-perception. Not only does it instill an inner calmness, but it also enables you to be more responsive than reactive in different scenarios.

It is very important to be able to regulate your thoughts and emotions so that you don't end up making the wrong decisions out of haste and a surge of feelings that you should have controlled. At first, you might not see any outward changes in yourself after practicing mindfulness and meditation. But with time, you will start to see the difference a few minutes of meditation are beginning to create in your life. It became apparent to me that I eventually grew accustomed to the serenity that resulted from my regular and sustained mindfulness practice. I started to value spending those reflective periods alone, thinking back on my life and developing a deeper, more profound connection with myself. Thus, these practices led me to find my inner peace and love.

When you break down inner peace and love into its components, you will see a unique connection between the mind and the heart. Inner peace is when you learn to regulate your thoughts, such as focusing on rational thoughts instead of deviating toward irrational ones. It frees your mind of unnecessary clutter, and you find it easier to concentrate on things in the present moment. You will have less impact from your past or situations yet to come, but your brain couldn't stop thinking about it earlier. You will learn to focus on the present and live your life to the fullest by experiencing each moment to its full potential.

On the other hand, love obtained through mindfulness is the essential self-love and self-care that no human should live without. Mindfulness and meditation help you realize how you care for yourself. Once you connect with yourself, you will find yourself embarking on a transformative journey of self-care that will lead to healthier choices, healthier decisions, and an investment in yourself. Understanding the importance of yourself and prioritizing your needs can go a long way in improving your life for the better.

Embarking on the Journey

The journey to mindfulness was a whole new experience for me as my life before it was going on an entirely different track. I joined the Navy at an early age to escape my small town and the turbulent environment. Life at home wasn't the best, as I had to go through abusive conditions, so at that time, joining the military felt like a good option for me. Back then, the only highlight I focused on was leaving my past life and serving the country instead to the best of my ability. However, the military training we were provided ended up distancing me from my emotions, which, combined with my upbringing, made my journey to mindfulness much longer than it could have been otherwise.

We were trained to minimize our emotions and feelings, taught to simply react and respond, and our lives were spun into order, structure, and discipline. While I served in the Navy, this training helped me achieve my targets successfully, but I discovered there was no programming to reaccept emotions and feelings once we transitioned out of our service.

Life while serving in the Navy was utter turmoil as I was away from the states and disconnected from the movement of society. I found myself spiraling further away from my emotions. Because if I started to feel, I would only feel pain, sorrow, suffering, and all other emotions that would make me wish to leave as soon as possible. Still, I had to do my duty, so I stayed, disconnecting myself from my feelings for that amount of time.

Many years after I returned and my service ended, I knew something significant was missing in my life. I realized that I had to reconnect with all those emotions I had forcefully shut out, but after so many years, it was indeed a long journey for me to discover myself and live for the first time as a man who was never able to earlier in life. I started to incorporate mindfulness and meditation into my life, opening myself up to inner development. It was as if I had found a staircase leading to my self-discovery. My journey was long and challenging, but I do not regret it, as it enabled me to face the shadows of my past and confront my present behaviors to lead me to a better tomorrow. My life was full of internal and external turmoil, but this journey of mindfulness enabled me to reach a state of tranquility.

I realized that positive change came from within as I continued to challenge my beliefs and values, and instead of repressing my feelings, I learned to accept them. Letting go of all the negativity that was holding me down and allowing the past resentments to flow away purified my soul and cleansed myself internally for the life ahead. Just like fresh water is circulated into stagnant water and clears it up, the approach to mindfulness stirred my stagnant soul and freshened it for accepting the upcoming events in my future.

Career Transitions and Entrepreneurial Challenges

My career transitioned from serving in the Navy to starting my professional life without downtime or separation. I recall leaving the Navy on April 16th, and from the next day, I was ready to work on choosing another profession. Perhaps it was an outcome of my military training that I couldn't bring myself to stay free for long. It was imperative that I quickly move after I made up my mind. When I had recently left the Navy, I was unaware of the importance of rest and self-care during these times of transition.

Now, with time, I have come to realize that transition is not just when we progress from one determined phase of life to another, such as a career switch or the transition from childhood to adulthood. I realized that our lives are full of these small transition points as we shift from one role to another. A good example of this is a husband or father transitioning into the role of an employee when he goes to work. Recognizing these key transition points in life is important because if you don't take moments to reflect and adjust, you can be caught in a bad scenario of how you respond to a situation because you're out of alignment with the current atmosphere.

The groundbreaking challenges you will have to face in this life are vast and overwhelming; I discovered it firsthand when I delved into the world of entrepreneurs. Any business that you are building from scratch requires sacrifice. To succeed, you have to stretch out your abilities, your mental fortitude, and the capacity to extend yourself for the belief and passion behind your business endeavor. In order to reach out, you have to reach into yourself first to analyze what you are offering.

This is where the entrepreneurial journey builds your character to be resilient. Being equipped with mindfulness and meditation allows you to deal with these entrepreneurial challenges of going from zero to an idea or from a concept on paper to bringing something to life. This journey becomes the entrepreneur's success, and it doesn't just end there. Instead, it's a continuous process of being engaged every day, following your passion.

But of course, achieving a work-life balance is equally important. You can separate from your work through mindfulness and meditation to go home and appreciate time away from work. Other activities include going for a walk, being in nature, self-regulating through breathing, yoga, and regular exercise. For me, it was the mindfulness and conscious awareness of why I was doing something that continued to allow me to separate the different roles of my life. Mindfulness enabled me to be aware of myself to such an extent that I learned exactly how to regulate my thought process and energy in any scenario. It helped me know exactly when I could be more creative and productive and how to regulate my other hours to be productive. This realization gave me power over my decisions, and I found it extremely helpful to balance my entrepreneurial and personal life.

The Unraveling of Personal Life

An unforeseen turn came to my life when my father passed away in 2018. I remember I was working on my third startup, and his loss struck me with a deep lesson. With his passing, I realized that we all had very little time on our hands and had no idea when that would expire. So, this realization helped me make the most of my time and start to pursue my passion and purpose.

My father's death and pondering over the fleeting quality of life triggered a sense of urgency relative to time. Time became the forefront of my life as I knew that I had to put my attention, my energy, and my focus to help solve an issue and create a positive impact.

As I was unaware when my time would expire, I needed to focus on my work and I needed to bring my ideas to life. My personal life had unraveled with my father's passing, but I was able to start sewing it back together, focusing on the things that mattered in life and being mindful of the scenarios I was in so that I could regulate my thoughts and energy accordingly.

Rediscovering the Inner Child

Another remarkable experience I had through mindfulness was the healing of my inner child. I had never considered it a possibility; in fact, I didn't even remember that some unresolved issues in my childhood were holding me back.

I was married to Irasema at this time and, in this process, adopted both of her children, one of whom was a son.   It was during my interactions with him that I found my inner child. Irasema explained to me that he represented my inner child. It dawned on me that I was rejecting those experiences with him where the areas I needed healed.

I saw a reflection of my inner child in my son, and as I interacted more with him, I found it helped in my inner growth and the healing of my inner child who wanted to be healed and touched.

Moments spent with my son led to deeper research within my own self that I hadn't engaged with most of my life. Through this experience, my inner child lived out in person and was able to start healing.

The Path to Mindful Living

"Mindfulness isn't difficult; we just need to remember to do it."

-Sharon Salzberg

Mindful living is basically being aware of your surroundings, the people around you, the things you experience, and the feelings you go through every day. If you take these few moments of your life to pause, reflect, and be aware of your surroundings, you will find yourself very much involved in your life, creating a positive difference.

You can use the transition moments in your life, such as the bus ride to work, to pause and reflect on your life. Or when you are sitting down to eat dinner or lunch, you can appreciate the moment by taking part in mindful activities. Focus on the food; as you eat, try to be aware of all the flavors mingling in your mouth. Think about the food and how it got there and went through a long process to finally be within your reach. This will help you be aware of the importance of the moment, and you will learn to cherish and appreciate it.

These practices enable you to take a few moments to periodically reconnect with yourself and what's around you and continue with your life.

I engage in continuous meditation. My daily rhythm involves both morning and evening routines, but throughout the day, I seamlessly incorporate mindfulness. Whether using my mala beads in meetings to reaffirm affirmations or integrating meditation into a walk outdoors, it's a fluid and constant practice, not confined to set moments. That's how I keep myself connected to my inner self. Being mindful becomes a continuation for me. Just like we don't breathe once, we continue to breathe for as long as we are alive; similarly, instead of fixing a time for mindfulness, I have incorporated it into my daily life and made it part and parcel of my existence. Thus, it's not a practice for me; it's a movement.

And once you embrace this movement, it will become a natural part of your existence.

Embracing Love and Compassion

Once you start being mindful of yourself and your life, you start to see yourself as a living soul that has just as much importance in the world as the other souls surrounding you. Through mindful living, I realized that I was something to everybody around me, but I couldn't become someone for myself.

The first time I realized this was when I was painting a wall. Throughout my life, I have painted several walls, but as I completed the painting, I realized that I had chosen the color for that wall on my own, without being guided or influenced by anyone. I chose that color because it was important to me. It was a mindful decision on my part and rendered a part of myself into that work. It made me realize that my choices had an impact and that I wasn't just a robot going about my life mechanically. There had to be a purpose behind my existence, a reason for my being alive.

I realized that in my life, each decision I made, consciousness, thought, awareness, and emotion were tied to it. I began to think about the meaning behind it. And just like that, it made me think about the love and compassion I offered to others. Similarly, I needed that love and affection for myself, too. It's probably easy to give, but it was very hard for me to receive love and recognize what it was in its true essence. But as I began to think more for myself and understand what I meant to myself, I was able to recognize it. Recognizing love and compassion made it easier for me to accept it as well as contribute to it. It made me accept that we're all moving on journeys and don't know what other people around us might be going through. Love is to give, and compassion is to understand. Here, my journey for mindfulness made me able to receive love and compassion as well.

The Power of Mindful Entrepreneurship

Mindful entrepreneurship is leading from a place of awareness and consciousness. Once you make mindful decisions for your company by taking into account how they will impact the people connected to it, you will realize the importance of making mindful decisions for yourself as well.

For example, taking time out to relax by going to the spa helped me rejuvenate myself and think much better for the benefit of my team, as I gave them the opportunity to relax and recreate as well.

Today, I am running an incredible startup that is associated with the public foundation as well. My experience has made me realize the importance of mindful entrepreneurship, which I try to incorporate into my startup. There are tons of challenges for me to face as an entrepreneur, including growing as a person, as an entrepreneur, and building and scaling a team. However, by being mindful of what's going on around me, I can meditate, be grateful, and self-regulate my thoughts, and so can you. Whether it is about managing a startup or your life, mindfulness can help you get through it.

The Ongoing Journey

"When I let go of what I am, I become what I might be. When I let go of what I have, I receive what I need."

-Lao Tzu

The quote above beautifully sums up the ongoing journey I have embarked on. I motivate you to join me on this mindful living path to enrich our lives with self-awareness and contention. By letting go of all the unnecessary clutter in our lives, we will be able to discover ourselves and find out what our hearts, minds, and souls truly need from us.

Starting the journey and bravely continuing it will help us figure ourselves out. Just like I discovered that my problem was reacting first and thinking about it later (rabbit mind), I worked on slowing myself down through meditation to respond to the situation and then react (turtle mind).

Similarly, you can have a lot of repressed emotions and feelings that need to be addressed before you figure out what you really want from your life.

So, you will have to start looking for it within yourself and evaluate it fully if you want to move on and make the most of your life. We can always improve, so we shouldn't be complacent; instead, we should keep looking for ways to make things better for ourselves and the people connected to us.

While we are on this journey, it feels like we are going deeper down into ourselves, but in reality, we are expanding, reaching further out, and evolving positively. We don't know what's behind the next door or the next step of our life. But as we get there, we are better prepared for it by being mindful of what we previously went through.

Chapter 2: Modern Day Story

"Never discourage anyone who continually makes progress, no matter how slow."

-Plato

Let's go back to the tale of the rabbit and the turtle to understand the benefits of mindfulness in life. Instead of breaking down the story this time, we will take a deep look into the characters of this fable and analyze the thought process behind their actions and the mindset that influences them to make certain decisions in life.

By doing so, we can better understand how mindfulness can help us achieve our targets. We will explore how the rabbit's impulsive and overconfident nature caused him to lose focus on the goal, while the turtle's steady and deliberate approach helped him stay focused on the task at hand.

You will notice that many people around us have mindsets similar to these two characters, which can be a strength or a weakness for them, depending on how they use it. There are exceptions to the rule, as slow and steady doesn't always win the race. In this fast-paced culture, we have to figure out the right approach to tackle our challenges by analyzing the context ourselves.

The Fast-Thinking Rabbit

The first character introduced in this tale was the rabbit, a clever, fast, but overconfident animal who thought winning a race with the turtle would be easy.

Being a fast creature who valued speed as his greatest asset, the rabbit was more instinctive than intuitive. When faced with a challenge, he reacted quickly, trying to overcome it. This suggests the rabbit followed the ideology of acting first and thinking later. He chose the first line of action he thought of without considering whether it was suitable for the task he wished to complete.

Speed might be his greatest asset, but finding quick solutions to the challenges he faced, he often overlooked the right way to solve the problem. As a result, he exhausted himself and got frustrated, losing the will to complete the task.

Furthermore, the rabbit was not as determined as the turtle to finish the race. He only accepted the challenge because it seemed easy, and he underestimated his competitor. Thus, the rabbit was overconfident and lacked humility, owing to his arrogance. His tendency to look at things at the surface level and judge based on appearance alone caused his defeat.

Having a mindset and behavior similar to the rabbit can lead us to face difficulties in life. In quickly deciding our line of action, we might overlook risk assessment or not have a plan B in case our approach fails to yield results. Abandoning tasks and never taking them to completion creates a lack of fulfillment, which might also dissuade us from selecting other tasks. In order to overcome these problems, we must embrace mindfulness to free ourselves of all the unnecessary clutter and restore our focus on the important things.

The Mindfulness Meditating Turtle

On the other hand, the turtle has a completely different mindset when compared to the rabbit. He knew the rabbit was faster than him but still accepted the challenge, determined to reach the finish line. His determination and consistency led him to win the race even though he was much slower than the rabbit.

The turtle was aware of his slow pace, but instead of viewing it as a weakness, he turned it into a strength, steadily pacing toward the finish line. The slow pace helped him not to get burned out in the first half of the race as he conserved his energy and kept heading toward his goal.

Moreover, the turtle knew the challenge he was taking and his strengths and weaknesses while addressing it. This suggests that the turtle implemented the ideology of thinking first and acting later. His actions were calculated and consistent, which could not have been possible if he had jumped right into the race without weighing out the pros and cons of taking the slow and steady approach.

Contrary to the rabbit, the turtle didn't just look at the surface of the problem. He delved deeper to understand the importance of endurance and used that trait as his strength. He did not get distracted during the race and steadily edged closer to the finish line, winning that apparently impossible race against the speedy rabbit.

Having a mindset and behavior similar to the turtle enables us to find the right approach to counter our challenges through meditation and careful thinking. Taking each step focused on our goal and being consistent helps us achieve the target and complete the challenge. Careful thinking before action also helps recognize the risks and their mitigation strategies. As a result, a person following this approach is more likely to succeed in his endeavors.

The Turtle and the Rabbit — Problem Solving

"Between stimulus and response, there is a space. In that space is our power to choose our response. In our response lies our growth and our freedom."

-Victor Frankl

Let's reconsider the story of the rabbit and turtle in the modern times. The fast-thinking rabbit and the mindfulness-meditating turtle were given the task of solving a puzzle rather than competing in a race. Here, the challenge was limited to using their mental capability, giving both a fair chance to win as no physical constraints held them back. There was only one solution to the puzzle, although multiple methods existed for a solution. However, careful thinking is required to select the right approach for the solution.

The rabbit was assured he would win that time and jumped into solving the puzzle without thinking much. He felt that if he went through all the methods he knew to solve it quickly, he would get the answer before the turtle even finished reading the questions.

The turtle, on the other hand, was a slow and steady thinker. He approached his thoughts with patience and mindfulness, observing the context before coming to a conclusion. He was not concerned with speed or agility but with understanding and wisdom. Therefore, no matter what task he was given, he carefully understood it first and then sorted out the ways to solve it.

Rushing to find the right answer, the rabbit overlooked a clue to solving the puzzle as he didn't read the question thoroughly. Despite going through several methods, he still couldn't find the answer. Frustrated, he abandoned the task, not realizing that the answer was in front of him the whole time.

Conversely, the turtle didn't miss that clue as he freed his mind from all the clutter through meditation and then focused on the question. When he started to solve the puzzle, it was much easier for him to apply the suitable method and find the correct answer. Thus, once again, the turtle proved that his slow but steady mindset helped him to win.

The rabbit learned a valuable lesson from the turtle that day. He realized that his fast and furious approach was not always the best way to solve problems. Sometimes, slowing down, thinking clearly, and acting mindfully was better. He also realized that he had underestimated the turtle, who had shown him the power of patience and concentration.

From that day onwards, the rabbit and the turtle developed a close friendship and collaborated regularly. Learning from each other, they worked together to solve problems innovatively, combining the rabbit's speed and agility with the turtle's mindfulness and wisdom.

Here, the rabbit and the turtle are character archetypes, having distinct traits and mindsets that enable them to approach the same puzzle differently. There is value in both approaches, depending on the problem that has to be solved. In some cases, speed is the right approach to finding the answer. In other cases, thoughtfulness and attention to detail.

Life Lessons from the Story

We all remember the moral of the rabbit and turtle's story: *Slow and steady wins the race.* But it wasn't the only thing that could be learned from the tale of the rabbit and the turtle. There were several important life lessons hidden in that simple children's fable that, if you incorporate them into your life, you will notice the remarkable changes it will bring.

1.   **Small Steps Can Lead You to Big Prizes:** Just like the small steps taken by the turtle led him to the finish line, your small steps to success can lead you to achieve your targets in life. The key is to be consistent and keep putting one foot after the other, continuing the race until you reach the finish line, no matter how long it takes. Progress comes from discipline; discipline comes in daily practice or habits accruing over time.

2.   **Success Needs an Objective:** You cannot achieve success if your targets are not defined first. Without a finish line marking the end of the race, you have no direction to put your efforts in. Thus, success without any target or objective you decide beforehand is impossible. Know what you have to achieve to work for it accordingly. Success is defined in the daily journey, not the arrival of a destination.

3.   **Never Give Up — Even When You Feel Like You Can't Keep Going Further:** The key aspect that made the turtle win the race was his determination. He didn't give up even though his competitor held an unfair advantage over him. Instead, he kept moving forward, step by step. Each step led him closer to the finish line (completing a task or simply taking the next step), and he eventually won the race through his consistency.

4.   **Success Requires Effort:** Without putting in the necessary effort, you can't expect yourself to succeed. Nothing comes easy in life; we must work hard to achieve any target or

goal. The more effort we put in to achieve our goal, the easier it will be to complete the task.

5.   Don't be Influenced by Others: Whether it is other people influencing you to deviate from your targets, your brain making excuses, or subjecting you to distractions, keep your eyes on the finish line and keep moving ahead. The rabbit stopped to take a nap because he thought the turtle wouldn't be able to catch up with him, and that one move cost him the race. Similarly, even the tiniest of negligence can set you off track and make reaching your target harder. So block out all those influences and keep moving toward your goal steadily.

6.   Don't Draw Comparisons Between Yourself and Other Seemingly More Successful People: Looking at people who are better off than us in life or career can serve as a motivation or a source of frustration. It depends on our mindset and how we handle the situation. If you have an optimistic mindset, you will look at their success as a source of motivation. But if you have a pessimistic mindset, you will draw comparisons and get frustrated as to why you couldn't achieve the same success as they did.

7.   Believe in Yourself: Half of the race is won if you believe you can win. If the turtle had refused to participate in the race, thinking he couldn't win from the rabbit, he wouldn't have won. Believe in yourself that you can do it no matter how hard the task is. With this positive mindset and belief in yourself, you can achieve anything you set your heart upon.

8.   Know Your Strengths and Weaknesses: Knowing your strengths and weaknesses enables you to use them to your advantage and select the right approach. The turtle knew it would take him longer to reach the finish line than the rabbit, but he knew his strength was determination. So he continued steadily, and while the rabbit took a nap break, the turtle passed him and won the race.

9.   Finish What You Have Started: It is no use to take part in a race if you're not going to finish it. Having a series of unfinished and abandoned projects will never give you the fulfillment of having completed the targets you have set in your life. It's never about the speed with which you achieve the targets; it's about finishing what you started.

Throughout this chapter, we have delved into several important factors crucial for success in life. First and foremost, consistency is key. Whether it's in our daily habits, routines, or work ethic, being consistent can help us stay focused and on track toward our goals.

In addition to consistency, determination is another important factor. The drive that keeps us going even when we face challenges or setbacks. It becomes the motivation that propels us forward toward our desired outcomes. Along with determination, believing in oneself gives us the confidence to take risks and push ourselves beyond our limits.

Mindfulness meditation is another tool that can be incredibly helpful in achieving success. Practicing mindfulness can cultivate greater awareness and clarity, which can help us make better decisions, stay focused, and reduce stress and anxiety.

Furthermore, we have explored the two opposing mindsets of the turtle and the rabbit. The turtle represents a slow and steady approach, while the rabbit embodies a more fast-paced strategy. By understanding the strengths and weaknesses of each mindset, we can determine which approach best suits our goals. Speed and endurance, when combined with a positive attitude, can help us achieve our goals easily.

Ultimately, life is a series of challenges we must overcome, targets we must achieve, and tasks we must complete. Our success heavily depends on how we approach these obstacles and the strategies we use to overcome them. By adopting the right attitude, staying determined, and utilizing the proper tools and resources, we can achieve our desired outcomes and live a fulfilling life.

Chapter 3: The Answer Is Within

"Mind, brain, and body make the man, and the man is capable of so much."

-Wilder Penfield

In all the challenges we wish to overcome, we either see ourselves lacking the right tools to complete the tasks or believe that our skill sets are far above those. As a result, we fail to achieve our targets due to a perception we form in our minds regarding them.

We often tend to look for external sources to provide us with a solution to the problems we are currently facing when, in reality, most of those answers are within ourselves. It depends on how we discover those answers and respond to our environment accordingly. The human brain and the mind are the most vital tools required for this process and understanding.

It is crucial to understand the roles of the brain and the mind in affecting human behavior and psychology before we proceed to explore what makes them different and how they are connected.

The Brain and the Mind

One of the body's primary organs, the brain, regulates every bodily function, including breathing, blood flow, food digestion, and energy production.

Without the brain, we cannot function properly, as seen in the cases of patients who suffer from a comatose state during which their brain shuts down and stops controlling normal bodily functions. Addiction and mental disorders also impact the brain's ability to govern our physical and mental functions.

On the other hand, the mind encompasses all your conscious experiences—your thoughts, feelings, emotions, memories, and perceptions. It's the intangible space where your sense of self resides. Think of it this way: the brain is the hardware, and the mind is the software that runs on it. Rene Descartes first gave the concept of mind through his quote, *"cogito ergo sum"* (I think therefore I am). Until the 17th century, the connection between the mind and brain was not explored. Descartes' work proposed that the mind was a distinct entity and was separate from the brain, marking a turning point in Western philosophy.[1] However, the concept of mind has evolved vastly since then.

We have now shifted to Brain 2.0 thinking, which suggests that we are not defined by our thoughts but are conscious observers of them. By being mindful of our thoughts, actions, and reactions, we can cultivate a greater sense of awareness and control.

---

[1] Hansotia, P. (2003). Understanding the difference between the mind and the brain. Nature; Springer Nature.
https://www.nature.com/articles/d41586-023-01017-w

The brain and mind are two terms often used interchangeably, but the question arises of whether the brain and the mind are similar or are two separate things that we mistakenly perceive to be the same.

Neuroscience investigates the relationship between the brain and the mind by studying brain structure, function, and neural activity. It explores how neural processes give rise to mental phenomena such as perception, cognition, emotions, and consciousness. Neuroscientists seek to understand how neural networks and neurotransmitters interact to produce various cognitive and behavioral functions by employing techniques like brain imaging, electrophysiology, and neuropsychology.

The key finding through neuroscience that differentiates the brain and the mind is that 'the mind uses the brain and responds to the mind.' The brain is a complex neuroplastic responder that can be influenced by our thoughts, decisions, and feelings, which constitute the major portion of the mind. Thus, the brain works as an instrument while the mind acts as an operator.[2]

Thus, the brain can be developed continuously through our mind—all the thoughts and feelings we feed into our brain

---

[2] Leaf, C. (2021). The Difference Between the Mind & Brain, Per A Neuroscientist. Mindbodygreen: Well-Rounded Well-Being for a Life Well Lived. https://www.mindbodygreen.com/articles/difference-between-mind-and-brain-neuroscientist

develop it in a certain way. Overloading the brain with too many thoughts simultaneously will cause it to freeze (rabbit mind), just like a computer processor with too many functions running. However, if we are mindful of the thoughts we send to our brain and focus on mental exercises and meditation, our brain will have more time to process each task and not go into a frenzy (turtle mind).

The Brain's Role in Decision Making

Our brain is responsible for decision-making just as much as it is responsible for transmitting signals to our body and causing it to function. It absorbs all the stimuli present in our environment, the internal and external sensations, our thoughts, and the emotions that are generated as a result of the given stimuli. The brain has a complex decision-making process, simplified into these four steps:

1. **Information Gathering:** Sensory organs send signals to the brain about the environment.

2. **Processing:** Different regions of the brain (mainly the prefrontal cortex and the hippocampus) analyze the information, drawing on past experiences and memories.

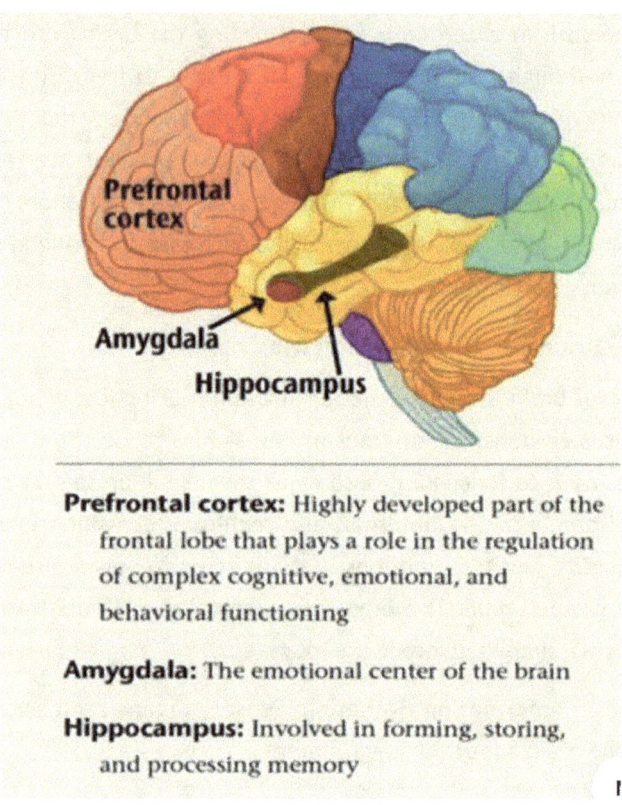

Prefrontal cortex: Highly developed part of the frontal lobe that plays a role in the regulation of complex cognitive, emotional, and behavioral functioning

Amygdala: The emotional center of the brain

Hippocampus: Involved in forming, storing, and processing memory

Image source:
https://www.pinterest.com/pin/182395853648821204/

3. **Evaluation:** The brain weighs options and potential consequences.

4. **Action:** The brain sends signals to the body to initiate a response. This action results from the decisions our brain makes based on the information it processes and evaluates.[3]

To understand this better, consider a simple example of choosing a restaurant to visit. Suppose you live in a town with three famous food chains. You have visited each of these restaurants before and have specific experiences and memories tied to them. Now that you are deciding which restaurant you should revisit, your brain will follow the process of decision-making discussed earlier:

Your brain will start to 'gather all the information' about restaurants A, B, and C. This information can be your personal experience, or it can also be a recommendation from a friend, an article by a food critic, a restaurant rating, etc. It will also gather sensory information, including the different sights, smells, sounds, tastes, and tactility you encounter.

Next, it will 'process' the information and link your memories to your experience while visiting the restaurant. Restaurant A served good food, but the environment was unpleasant due to the lack of lighting and poor service. Restaurant B was visually pleasing, but the food was not good.

---

[3] Brocas, I. (2023). Exploring Brain Processes During Basic Decision-Making. Psychology Today.
https://www.psychologytoday.com/intl/blog/biology-development-and-behavior/202310/exploring-brain-processes-during-basic-decision-making

Restaurant C had an average design and ambiance, but you enjoyed the food served there.

Based on these memories, the brain can 'evaluate' whether you had a good or a bad experience. It will also assess how likely you are to visit the restaurant again. From the above example, it is clear that you had a comparatively better experience at Restaurant C.

Finally, the brain selects one of the three restaurants based on the experience and memories as well as the taste and quality of the food, which in this example happens to be C. This selection is the 'action' resulting from your decision.[4]

Neuroscientists have discovered that the brain's prefrontal cortex is mainly responsible for this decision-making process. It is also known as the area for rational thinking, which plays its part each time you decide, whether it is as simple as choosing what to wear or as complex as solving a mathematics equation. Thus, the prefrontal cortex carries out all the activity in the four steps of decision-making. In contrast, the hippocampus (part of the brain responsible for storing memories) provides the memories and experiences needed for evaluation.[5]

---

[4] Hathaway, B. (2019). How the brain helps us make good decisions — and bad ones. YaleNews. https://news.yale.edu/2019/06/25/how-brain-helps-us-make-good-decisions-and-bad-ones

[5] Moghadem, S. S., Khodadad, F. S., & Khazaeinezhad, V. (2019). An Algorithmic Model of Decision Making in the Human Brain. PubMed Central (PMC).

Impact of Mindfulness on Decision-Making

Now that you know how the brain makes decisions based on sensory information and memories, as well as the crucial part responsible for decision-making (the prefrontal cortex), we will discuss mindfulness's impact on our brains' ability to make good decisions.

The story of the rabbit and the turtle clearly demonstrates the difference between their mindsets and how it led them to make different decisions. The rabbit was jumping from one solution to the other, which overloaded his brain, and he couldn't notice the clue to the solution right in front of him. As a result, he decided to abandon the task, which restricted him from achieving the target. On the other hand, the turtle paused to think, practiced mindful meditation, and arrived at the correct solution. He found the clue and reached the answer by making the right decision, giving his brain time to evaluate and select the possible solution.

So, what impact did that mindful meditation have on the turtle?

When the turtle paused to meditate, his brain went through the following changes:

---

https://www.ncbi.nlm.nih.gov/pmc/articles/PMC7149951/#:~:text=It%20is%20well%20known%20that,of%20action%20still%20are%20unknown.

Creation of Space in the Prefrontal Cortex: Mindful meditation frees your brain of all the unnecessary clutter, creating space in the prefrontal cortex. As this region of the brain is responsible for decision-making, expelling unwanted thoughts and information will help it function better.

Improved Blood Flow: Breathing in and out for regulated amounts of time improves your blood flow to the brain. Blood is a vitalizing agent for all the organs in the human body, so the more blood flows into the brain, the better it will perform.

Reduced Stress: Meditation helps to reduce stress by regulating breathing patterns and heartbeat. It programs your brain to slow down, think, and respond, reducing the stress of having to act instantly.

Increased Focus and Concentration: Mindfulness and meditation techniques improve cognitive functions and help focus and maintain concentration.

These changes helped the turtle to pause and analyze the situation with a relaxed mind, enabling his brain to make a good decision.

Similarly, applying mindfulness meditation to our daily lives can help us immensely by reducing all the negativity and clutter that weighs us down and enabling our brains to function better.

Brain Fatigue

We suffer from brain fatigue when we overload our brains with multiple thoughts, tasks, or ideas (like the rabbit did in the story). Also known as mental exhaustion or brain fog, it occurs after prolonged mental exertion, and our brain starts to feel foggy, lags in processing things, and impacts us on a physical and psychological level.

This mental exhaustion can affect any person, regardless of age, gender, or genetics. The following factors are responsible for causing brain fatigue:

Depleted Resources: The brain relies on energy from glucose and oxygen. When these resources are depleted, our concentration and focus can suffer.

Information Overload: Constant thinking and multitasking bombard the brain, leading to feeling overwhelmed.

Emotional Stress: Emotional states can significantly impact our cognitive abilities, causing brain fatigue.

When one or more of these factors impact your brain, it affects your productivity and performance, leading your brain to shut down after exhaustion. You cannot work, focus, or rest properly, adversely impacting your physical and mental well-being.

If you are experiencing any of the symptoms listed below, chances are that you are also suffering from brain fatigue:

- Loss of mental energy during or after work

- Inability to focus or maintain concentration

- Headaches and stress

- Light and sound sensitivity

- Temporary loss of certain memories

- Inability to sleep or insomniac behavior

These symptoms, and more, indicate that your brain is getting exhausted by the increasing burden of thoughts and information. Therefore, you might need to take a moment to slow down, regulate your breathing, and give your brain a break. Mindfulness practices like meditation can help us manage these factors. Focusing our attention and calming our emotions can improve our cognitive stamina and enhance our decision-making abilities.[6]

The Brain-Mind Connection

As discussed earlier, the brain and mind are interconnected because one cannot function without the other. The brain generates the physical basis for our mental experiences, while our thoughts and emotions influence the way our brain functions.

---

[6] Jacquet, T., and Lepers, R. (2023). Mental Fatigue: What Happens When Your Brain Is Tired? Young Minds. 11:1080802. Doi: 10.3389/frym.2023.1080802

For example, chronic stress can alter brain structure and function, while mindfulness practices can promote neuroplasticity, defined as the brain's ability to change and adapt. In both these instances, the brain and the mind are working together.

Understanding this connection is key to cultivating mindfulness. The future of psychotherapy practices depends on exploring and improving the brain-mind connection. What we feed into our brains through our minds in the form of thoughts, emotions, and sensory information leads to either good decision-making or brain fatigue, depending on how we feed the data.[7]

When our brain is overworked, it becomes fatigued and negatively affects both our mental and physical abilities. Our mental processes will be enhanced, and space in the prefrontal cortex of our brains will be created if we meditate and carefully choose the information required for a single decision. This will enable us to work more effectively without becoming more and more fatigued.

---

[7] Barrett, L. F. (2009). The Future of Psychology: Connecting Mind to Brain - PMC. PubMed Central (PMC). https://www.ncbi.nlm.nih.gov/pmc/articles/PMC2763392/

Chapter 4: The Rabbit Mind

"A cluttered mind makes for a cluttered life."

-Anonymous

With the mind-blowing inventions and technological advancements of the 21st century, our world has become increasingly fast-paced. As a result, life has become more complex, and every individual is engrossed in the race to succeed. From schools to workplaces and even at home, we are juggling multiple tasks simultaneously within a short time, trying to overcome the overwhelming competition we face. In our constant attempts to achieve our targets faster, we tend to fail fast as well, starting a task and abandoning it just as quickly if it doesn't work out for us.

Humans are heavily geared toward competition. Thus, every action we take is accompanied by a variety of thoughts. *Will it hurt me or benefit me? Should I invest my time into this task or move on? Perhaps it will neither hurt nor benefit me, but I can still perform it to be certain.* All these thoughts and more burden our brains with every passing second, and the competition around us forces us to take up more than one task at a time. The more tasks there are, the more questions arise in our brains, which eventually causes us to slow down and abandon the current task to focus on another. This chapter discusses the rabbit mind, which refers to this cycle of trying to manage multiple tasks and failing faster to restart all over again. We will discuss the race from the rabbit's perspective, the rabbit mindset in detail, the various multitasking traps we set ourselves up to, and the consequences we face.

The Race — Rabbit's Perspective

The rabbit challenged the turtle to a race on a warm, sunny day. The slowest creature in the forest being challenged by one of the fastest seemed no less than a joke. *After all, what competition could exist between the rabbit who could hop for miles and a turtle who took hours to cover the same distance?* The mere idea of a race between these two was nothing short of absurd.

The rabbit presumed it would be effortless to win from the turtle. True, if he had been competing against the cheetah or the red fox, that would have been a worthy challenge. Even the monkey who lazed away all day was faster than the turtle if the reward was a cluster of bananas at the end. The turtle was so slow that the rabbit was certain he could cross the finish line thrice in the time it would take him to reach once.

But the challenge had already been accepted, and the rabbit was ready to win by all means. All the jungle animals were gathered for the spectacle, and a path was decided upon, with a finish line marking its end.

"Rabbit! Rabbit! Rabbit!"

The crowd's cheers fueled his adrenaline, and he landed at the starting line with one agile hop. The turtle was slowly inching closer to the line, and seeing him, the rabbit couldn't help but stifle a laugh.

At last, the turtle reached, and the tension in the atmosphere soared. Both animals got into position, awaiting the signal to start the race. The elephant contracted its trunk and bellowed loudly, furnishing the much-awaited signal.

The rabbit was off like a bullet piercing through the air, leaving excited gasps of the bystanders in his wake. The wind whipped through his fur as he sped across the forest, the trees, flowers, and animals reduced to only a smear of color.

He was going to win the race without a shadow of a doubt. With his exhilarating speed, he had already crossed half of the path, and the turtle was nowhere in sight. His nimble legs came to a halt in the clearing, and he turned to judge if his opponent was anywhere close by.

But as expected, the turtle was far behind, and not even a speck of dust or a sound of crunching leaves could hint at his slow arrival.

The rabbit stretched his legs and took a short break. His thoughts were rushing just like he had been blazing through the path a few seconds earlier. The rabbit thought *the turtle would need some time to catch up with me so I could simply take a break and relax. I will still be ahead of the slowcoach when I start up again.*

The sound of fresh water caught his attention, and he skipped leisurely over to the nearby stream. Filling his palms with water, he quenched his thirst and felt refreshed. He could resume the race as he had rested enough, but his thoughts deviated shortly afterward.

It hadn't been long since he had stopped to take a break. He could rest more as the turtle would still be miles behind. The patch of clovers growing close to the stream felt quite enticing as well, so he decided to take a nibble or two.

He ate to his heart's content, and the turtle was still nowhere to be seen. Of course, it wasn't easy for such a slow creature to cover the vast distance the rabbit had easily hopped over. There was plenty of time left.

After eating, the rabbit started to feel quite sleepy. The race had not worn him out. He could actually travel twice as far with ease.

But the calm atmosphere, the cool breeze, and the contention that he was still way ahead of his opponent lulled him to sleep.

It's just a short nap. I can wake up in a short while and easily cover the gap, he convinced himself, nestled comfortably under the tree as he went to sleep.

That was where it all went wrong.

By the time the rabbit woke from his peaceful slumber, the sun was sinking below the horizon. Hours had lapsed, and panic gripped him as he jolted awake. *Oh no, I am late. I am too late!*

Frantic, he bolted through the landscape, the finish line looming into view. But the crowd was already cheering, much to his shock. When he reached, he saw that the line had already been crossed by none other than the slow but steady turtle.

The animals celebrated and lifted the turtle up to proclaim his victory. The rabbit's ears drooped in humiliation, and he slunk to the side, unable to accept his defeat. But deep down, he knew he was at fault for his defeat.

He had underestimated the turtle and gotten distracted during the race. He was so confident about winning that he never considered his strategy. So, the fact that he lost was quite justified.

The race, meant to be a display of his prowess, had turned into a humbling lesson. He realized with a heavy heart that speed wasn't everything. Focus, perseverance, and perhaps a healthy dose of respect for the opponent helped the turtle win the race, even though he was the slowest creature in the forest competing against the speedy rabbit.

What Is the Rabbit Mind?

The rabbit mind is a symbolic representation of how we act in our fast-paced lives. It is both a product and a cause of the staggering competition that exists today in each field, as every person is out there to prove their guts and take down their opponents by any means possible. However, in much of life our main competitor is ourselves, not someone else.

In this continuously evolving world, life has become a race, and we are rabbits trying to reach the finish line by hopping as fast as we can. To finish first, we only prioritize reaching the goal and do not focus on the journey (also known as having a reward-focused approach). As a result, we often face failure, after which we try another approach, then another, and so on until our brain gets exhausted and comes to an abrupt halt.

This process of jumping from one act to another instantly without pausing to think is a characteristic of the rabbit mindset. While working, we deal with multiple tasks at once and can eventually not focus on even a single task we selected. This continuous multitasking makes it seem like we always have work to do, and our brains do not get enough time to relax and rejuvenate.

Multitasking Traps

Multitasking is defined as performing more than one task at the same time. Similarly, multitasking traps refer to situations or habits that lead you to believe you are being productive by juggling multiple tasks simultaneously. However, balancing multiple tasks affects your focus and efficiency while also having severe consequences for your mental health.

Some of the common multitasking traps that you might have experienced in your life at one point or the other are discussed below:

Overestimation of Abilities: People often overestimate their ability to multitask effectively, believing they can handle multiple tasks simultaneously without a decrease in performance. This makes them take up more tasks than they can manage, eventually resulting in early burnout and brain fatigue.

Task Switching Costs: Each time the brain switches between tasks, a cognitive cost is associated with refocusing your attention and context switching. Context switching occurs when you pause an ongoing task and focus on another one. As a result, your brain has to shift gears and lose its concentration immediately, which can later lead to mistakes and burnout (also known as the costs of context switching). These costs can accumulate and lead to reduced efficiency and productivity.[8]

Pressure to Perform: In fast-paced work environments, you might experience pressure to multitask to meet deadlines or handle competing demands. This pressure can lead individuals to multitask even when it is not the most effective

---

[8] Sparrow, S. (2022). The surprisingly high cost of multitasking (and how to avoid it) | LeadDev. The Home of Engineering Leadership | LeadDev. https://leaddev.com/productivity-eng-velocity/surprisingly-high-cost-multitasking-and-how-avoid-it

approach. In 2010, a study conducted by Paridon and Kaufmann proved that multitasking in the workplace can lead to increased errors, accidents, and mental strain. This highlights the importance of creating an environment that allows employees to minimize distractions and concentrate on the task at hand instead of multitasking.[9]

Cultural Norms: In some cultures or rapidly progressing industries, multitasking may be viewed as a sign of productivity or efficiency, leading individuals to adopt multitasking behaviors as a way to demonstrate competence. Cultures emphasizing a stronger work ethic might appreciate people who multitask, viewing them as humans making full use of their brains. However, you only use 10-20% of your brain, regardless of how many tasks you are cramming in. Therefore, the more tasks you handle, the more your brain will likely freeze out of stress.[10]

Consequences of Multitasking on the Brain

Aside from burnout and brain fatigue, there are several negative consequences of multitasking on the brain. Research

---

[9] Paridon, H. M., & Kaufmann, M. (2010). Multitasking in work-related situations and its relevance for occupational health and safety: Effects on performance, subjective strain and physiological parameters. Europe's Journal of Psychology.
https://ejop.psychopen.eu/index.php/ejop/article/view/226/226.pdf

[10] Multitasking: The Efficiency Trap | by The Purple Writer | Be Unique. (2020). Medium. https://medium.com/be-unique/multitasking-the-efficiency-trap-94073d04287

shows that multitasking affects our performance and memory, making it a harmful factor that we willingly add to our lives without knowing the costs that come with it. We tend to make more mistakes, lose focus, and retain less information, changing how our brains work. This type of neuroplasticity is harmful to the brain as it is limiting our attention span and causing us to experience burnout earlier.[11]

Some of the negative consequences of multitasking are discussed below:

Reduced Efficiency: Multitasking often decreases overall productivity and efficiency as the brain constantly switches between tasks.

Decreased Quality of Work: Dividing attention among multiple tasks can compromise the quality of work produced. Mistakes are more likely to occur when attention is divided, leading to errors and inaccuracies.

Increased Stress: Juggling multiple tasks can increase stress levels as the brain struggles to meet competing demands. This can lead to feelings of overwhelming anxiety, which leads to mental strain.

Impaired Decision Making: Multitasking can impair decision-making abilities as the brain may not have enough

---

[11] Madore, K. P., & Wagner, A. D. (2019). Multicosts of Multitasking. PubMed Central (PMC).
https://www.ncbi.nlm.nih.gov/pmc/articles/PMC7075496/

time to evaluate each option or fully consider the consequences of choices. Decisions taken in haste might not be suitable for achieving the target and further slow the task completion process.

Strained Relationships: Multitasking can negatively impact relationships by making individuals appear distracted or disinterested when communicating with others. This can lead to misunderstandings and feelings of neglect among spouses, children, family members, and friends.

Loss of Creativity: Dividing attention among multiple tasks can inhibit creative thinking and problem-solving abilities, as the brain may not have the opportunity to engage in deep, focused thought processes. The brain prioritizes only finishing as many tasks as possible and neglects the quality of the tasks, which affects the creative process.

Fragmented Attention: Multitasking also results in fragmented attention, preventing individuals from fully engaging with a particular task. This can lead to shallow processing and reduced comprehension.

Inability to Prioritize: Multitaskers find it difficult to prioritize tasks effectively, leading them to focus on less important tasks at the expense of more critical ones.

Distractions: Multitasking often involves exposure to distractions such as notifications, emails, calls, social media, or colleague interruptions. These distractions can further fragment attention and disrupt workflow.

Lack of Time Management Skills: Poor time management skills can contribute to multitasking as individuals attempt to juggle multiple tasks without adequately allocating time.

Physical Health Impacts: Constantly switching between tasks can lead to increased levels of stress hormones in the body, which can have detrimental effects on physical health over time, such as elevated blood pressure and weakened immune function.

The rabbit mind is characterized by multitasking and rapidly jumping from one thought to another. While it may seem that you are at the peak of your productivity by performing multiple tasks in rapid succession, in reality, you are overloading your brain, making it impossible to focus on each task particularly.

As a result, people with rabbit minds get involved too much but can't complete their tasks due to a lack of concentration and efficiency.

In the race to finish first, they fail repeatedly, which ultimately causes them to give up. Their mental health also gets affected, leading to feelings of frustration, discouragement, and even anxiety.

However, having the rabbit mindset is not a fixed personality trait. Your brain and mind are not machines; therefore, you should stop treating them as such and incorporate relaxation and stress management into your busy life as well. With awareness, effort, and mindfulness meditation, you can learn to manage your thought process and achieve greater focus, leading to a more productive and fulfilling life.

Chapter 5: The Turtle Mind

"Slowing down your thoughts on a regular basis is the path to consistent peace of mind."

-Amy Leigh Mercree

In the never-ending race of human life, there are two types of people: those focused on the reward and the journey. The cycle continues as the race to one target ends and the race to another starts, but these types of people react very differently to their challenges.

As we discussed, the rabbit has a reward-focused approach, looking only for the outcome, not the process. However, the turtle's mindset is opposite to that of the rabbit, as he focuses on the journey and lives in the moment. While the rabbit keeps rushing, the turtle slows down and takes in each moment, making life worthwhile.

Similarly, people who have a rabbit mindset set all their focus on the end, while those with a turtle mindset slow down, collect their thoughts, and respond to the challenge instead of just reacting to it.

But in this competitive world, where every person is engrossed in a race, is it worth it to slow down and take a break?

Slowing down is a fear for most people, as they think they will be left behind. So, in their race to the finish line, they miss out on all the meaningful things that would have made their experience much more memorable. And when they finally achieve their target, the accomplishment doesn't feel worth their effort. It seems something important is still missing because they rushed through the process and couldn't retain it as a worthwhile experience.

This chapter discusses the turtle mind, which refers to slowing down and responding to the current situation effectively. We will discuss the race from the turtle's perspective, the turtle mindset in detail, the importance of mindful transitions, and some effective techniques to help us slow down.

The Race—Turtle's Perspective

When news spread of the turtle and the rabbit participating in a race, everyone knew who would win. The rabbit had nimble legs that could easily hop over long distances, while the turtle had small, round feet, weighed down already by the heavy shell on his back. It wasn't hard to guess which one of the two would be able to cross the finish line first.

The turtle could hear the excited whispers of the animals, who were confident that he would lose. The entire forest had gathered to watch the race, and most animals were putting their bets on the rabbit to win. After all, it seemed like the only logical end to the race, as the rabbit was one of the fastest creatures, and the turtle had already taken half an hour to get to the clearing where the race was organized.

But the turtle didn't let those whispers and mocking laughter hold him down. He knew he hadn't challenged his opponent to that race just to win. He had a much greater purpose in mind.

He wanted to show the rabbit that speed wasn't always the right approach. Sometimes, clear thinking and consistency can overcome the toughest of challenges.

"Rabbit! Rabbit! Rabbit!"

The crowd was cheering for the rabbit when he inched closer to the starting line, taking each step carefully. Even his brethren were looking at him with wide, pitiful eyes as if the race's fate had already been decided.

The rabbit was waiting at the starting line, and he gave him a haughty look as if he could already imagine himself winning the cup. It must have seemed like an easy challenge to the rabbit, who could hop over miles without getting tired.

At last, the signal was given, and the race began. With the speed of a bullet, the rabbit whizzed past and disappeared shortly after. The cheers turned deafening as the animals were sure he would reach the finish line much earlier than the poor turtle, moving step by step.

But the turtle steadily kept going, willing himself to focus on the journey ahead of him. A long path was laid out, and he had to be mindful of his energy throughout the race. He couldn't let himself burn out soon if he wished to win.

Slow and steady, slow and steady, the turtle repeated that mantra as he kept moving forward despite the obstacles he faced. Even if the rabbit had possibly crossed the finish line, the turtle was determined to get to the end. He would not leave the race in the middle and willed himself to keep going, kicking the stones out of his way and thinking about each move he had to make.

Halfway through, he reached a calm lake that flowed alongside the path chosen for the race. After careful consideration and being mindful of the time left, the turtle decided to swim through the lake instead of slowly crossing the path on land. Thus, he rolled inside his shell, throwing himself into the water. With the current approach more suited to his nature, he covered much more distance than he could have on land, and by the time he came out of the water, he saw that the sun was slowly dipping over the horizon.

Surprisingly, he found the rabbit curled up by a bush and fast asleep. A smile spread on his face as he didn't pause but kept moving ahead, victory finally seeming in his grasp.

I can do it, he whispered, motivating himself to complete the last few miles as well. While the rabbit slept unaware, the turtle reached the clearing.

After waiting for so long, most of the crowd of animals dispersed, but seeing the turtle approach, they burst into shocked cheers and applause. Who would have thought that the turtle would end up defeating the rabbit? But the impossible had been achieved, and the race winner was the turtle, one of the slowest creatures in the forest.

The rabbit was severely humiliated and unsure of how to respond when he eventually showed up, looking unkempt and gasping in shock that the turtle had prevailed. But after giving it some thought, he realized how weak his plan was in comparison to his opponent's. The turtle's perseverance enabled him to defeat a foe who was twice as quick as him, but the rabbit's conceit had finally caught up with him. What is the turtle mind?

The turtle mind is a symbolic representation of how a person fully aware of his surroundings and in perfect control of his mind reacts to everyday situations. Instead of rushing through each task, he pauses to think, collects his thoughts, chooses the right method, and then deals with his challenges.

A person with this mindset does not focus on the outcomes but on the process that eventually leads to the desired result. Therefore, he responds to his challenges rather than just reacting to them. Each move he makes is thought out, and he doesn't get tired of rushing from one method to the next, as he is able to select the right one after carefully pondering and weighing out the pros and cons.

The turtle mind is calm and serene, a perfect implementation of mindfulness meditation to deal with life's challenges. Such a person slows down his thoughts and is very synchronized with his mind and body, picking up the right approaches to implement according to his targets. He is focused and does not get distracted, which makes him productive and efficient. It also helps him achieve his goals more effectively than those with a rabbit mindset.

Slowing Down Your Thoughts

The first step to achieving a turtle mindset is to slow down your thoughts and reflect. It might seem hard after years of being accustomed to multitasking and rushing through life, but once you are determined enough to change your life's course, you will also succeed in changing your mindset.

Slowing down your thoughts is important because it can help you reduce stress, increase self-awareness, and improve mental health. Here are some ways in which slowing down your thoughts can be beneficial:

Slowed-down thoughts: When you slow down your thoughts, you reduce the amount of information your brain is processing, and as a result, you focus on one task at a time. This helps to reduce feelings of being overwhelmed and stressed by the tasks you must complete.[12]

Improved self-awareness: Slowing down your thoughts can help you become more aware of your emotions and feelings, allowing you to connect with yourself on a deeper

---

[12] Cohen, S., Kamarck, T., & Mermelstein, R. (1983). A Global Measure of Perceived Stress. Journal of Health and Social Behavior, 4, 385. https://doi.org/10.2307/2136404

level. It also helps to better understand yourself and your behavior in the different experiences of life.[13]

Enhanced mental health: Racing thoughts can be a symptom of anxiety and depression, and slowing down your thoughts can help reduce the severity of these symptoms. It has a positive impact on your mental health, too, as you learn to calm down and focus instead of rushing around and losing track of your thoughts.[14] Research has shown that mindfulness meditation can improve mental health outcomes by as much as 18%.[15]

Increased focus and productivity: When you slow down your thoughts and focus on one task at a time, you improve your ability to concentrate and be more productive. It helps you avoid all those multitasking traps that would later lead to brain fatigue.[16]

According to a meta-analysis published in the Journal of the American Medical Association, mindfulness-based therapies

---

[13] Kabat-Zinn, J. (2013). Full Catastrophe Living, Revised Edition: How to Cope with Stress, Pain and Illness Using Mindfulness Meditation. Bantam.

[14] American Psychological Association. (2013). Diagnostic and Statistical Manual of Mental Disorders, 5th Edition. American Psychiatric Publishing, Inc. http://dx.doi.org/10.1176/appi.books.9780890425596.893619

[15] Mrazek, M. D., Franklin, M. S., Phillips, D. T., Baird, B., & Schooler, J. W. (2013). Mindfulness training improves working memory capacity and GRE performance while reducing mind wandering. Psychological science, 24(5), 776-781.

[16] Berman, M. G., Jonides, J., & Kaplan, S. (2008). The Cognitive Benefits of Interacting with Nature. Psychological Science, 12, 1207–1212. https://doi.org/10.1111/j.1467-9280.2008.02225.x

are highly effective at reducing symptoms of anxiety by 39% and symptoms of depression by 32%[17]. This demonstrates that slowing down thoughts and cultivating mindfulness can help reduce feelings of stress and anxiety, improve focus and concentration, and promote relaxation. Therefore, it is the best tool to convert your mindset from the rabbit mindset to a turtle mindset through meditation, mindfulness, and some easy mind-calming techniques to change your life.[18]

Mindful Transitions

Transitions are defined as the process or period of changing from one state or condition to another. These are an important aspect of a person's life and occur throughout the day, particularly when leaving home, going to and from work, and managing different roles such as being a husband, father, and co-worker.

These transitions require individuals to shift their focus and adapt to new situations and roles, and they can significantly impact your overall well-being and work-life balance. Here are some reasons why transitions are important:

---

[17] Goyal, M., Singh, S., Sibinga, E. M., Gould, N. F., Rowland-Seymour, A., Sharma, R., ... & Ranasinghe, P. D. (2014). Meditation programs for psychological stress and well-being: a systematic review and meta-analysis. JAMA internal medicine, 174(3), 357-368.

[18] Khoury, B., Lecomte, T., Fortin, G., Masse, M., Therien, P., Bouchard, V., Chapleau, M.-A., Paquin, K., & Hofmann, S. G. (2013). Mindfulness-based therapy: A comprehensive meta-analysis. Clinical Psychology Review, 6, 763–771. https://doi.org/10.1016/j.cpr.2013.05.005

1. Maintaining balance: Transitions help individuals maintain balance by allowing them to separate different aspects of their lives, such as work and home life. By making a deliberate effort to transition between different roles, you can ensure that you give each role the attention it deserves and avoid burnout.

2. Coping with change: Transitions can also help individuals cope with changes in their lives, such as starting a new job or becoming a parent. By acknowledging and preparing for these new developments in life in that transition period, where you reevaluate and reflect on your thoughts, you can reduce stress and anxiety and adapt more effectively to new situations.

3. Improving focus: By setting aside time to transition between tasks or roles, you can clear your mind and refocus your attention, leading to better performance, increased concentration, and desired results.

4. Promoting self-care: Transitions can also allow you to engage in self-care activities, such as meditation, exercise, or hobbies. By taking time for yourself during transitions, you can enjoy life despite your busy schedule and live in the present moment.

The short periods when you are transitioning from one role to another can become a critical time frame for you to focus on your mental health. Do not rush through them. Take a moment to pause and reflect, gather your thoughts, and create space in your prefrontal cortex by breathing deeply. Thus, these transitions will become an energy-fueling period for your brain while you relax, accept your role, and slowly mold yourself.

Mind Calming Techniques

Many techniques can be used to calm the mind and reduce stress. Here are some effective techniques that you can use to slow down your thoughts and rejuvenate your mind:

1. Mindfulness meditation: This technique involves focusing on the present moment and observing your thoughts without judgment. It can help reduce stress and improve well-being. It also heals you internally when you release all the negativity through meditation and accept a state of calm and contention.[19]

2. Deep breathing: Deep breathing techniques, such as diaphragmatic breathing, can help to reduce stress and anxiety by slowing down the heart rate and promoting relaxation. It is also an effective technique for improving your sleep pattern and has a lasting positive impact on your mind and body.[20]

---

[19] Khoury, B., Sharma, M., Rush, S. E., & Fournier, C. (2015). Mindfulness-based stress reduction for healthy individuals: A meta-analysis. Journal of Psychosomatic Research, 6, 519–528.
https://doi.org/10.1016/j.jpsychores.2015.03.009
[20] Jerath, R., Edry, J. W., Barnes, V. A., & Jerath, V. (2006). Physiology of long pranayamic breathing: Neural respiratory elements may provide a mechanism that explains how slow deep breathing shifts the autonomic nervous system. Medical Hypotheses, 3, 566–571.
https://doi.org/10.1016/j.mehy.2006.02.042

3.   Progressive muscle relaxation: Progressive muscle relaxation involves tensing and relaxing different muscle groups in the body. This technique reduces physical tension and promotes relaxation throughout your body.

4.   Yoga: An exercise combining physical postures with breathing and meditation techniques, yoga helps to reduce stress and promote relaxation. It improves your physical and mental health, making you better equipped to deal with the problems you face in daily life.

5.   Visualization: Visualization involves imagining a peaceful scene or experience as part of a meditative session where you can let go of all your stress and worries. It is a highly effective relaxation technique and helps enrich your meditative experience.

A review of 47 studies found that mindfulness meditation, deep breathing, progressive muscle relaxation, and yoga were all effective in reducing symptoms of anxiety and depression.

In short, your mind needs to relax, too, as it is rushing through the daily aspects of life, keeping you active and functional. You must take care of it in return by slowing down your thoughts, practicing mindfulness meditation, and going through your life transitions thoughtfully. If you adopt these habits, you will successfully change your rabbit mindset into a turtle mindset and observe its many benefits for your overall well-being firsthand.

Chapter 6: Mindfulness

"Mindfulness is not about changing the world, but about learning to see it clearly."

-Rick Hansen, Ph.D.

As evident from the tale of the rabbit and the turtle, the only reason the slowest creature of the forest was able to win the race from the fastest creature was the awareness of the present. The turtle knew he couldn't outrun the rabbit, but he kept consistent and made a conscious decision to choose the river path as it was a better alternative.

On the other hand, the rabbit got distracted and was overconfident that he would win the race, making him waste time in a nap. Here, we see how the turtle's mindset helped him win, but how did he achieve that mindset? Can we also change our mindset from the overthinking rabbit to the mindful meditating turtle?

Yes, we can. This chapter will discuss the most crucial tool needed to transform our mindset: *Mindfulness*. We will look at what it means and how it impacts your brain. Furthermore, we will discuss tips for practicing mindfulness daily and an effective mindfulness exercise to improve your overall well-being.

What Is Mindfulness?

Mindfulness is the practice of being present and fully engaged in the current moment without judgment or distraction. All your thoughts converge to the present instead of deviating from other distracting actions. It enables you to be fully aware and in control of your present mental space as you intentionally direct your attention to your thoughts, feelings, and physical sensations in the present moment without getting caught up in past regrets or future worries.

This state of mind can be practiced through various techniques, such as meditation, deep breathing, body scans, or mindful movement. By focusing on the present moment and observing thoughts and emotions without judgment, you can increase self-awareness, reduce stress and anxiety, improve concentration and focus, and enhance overall well-being.

In clinical psychology, the most commonly used definition for mindfulness is given by Jon Kabat-Zinn, the founder of the Mindfulness-Based Stress Reduction program. He defines it as *"paying attention in a particular way: on purpose, in the present moment, and non-judgmentally."* He further explains that mindfulness is the awareness that arises through paying attention on purpose, in the present moment, and non-judgmentally.[21]

---

[21] Kabat-Zinn, J. (2003). Mindfulness-based interventions in context: Past, present, and future. Clinical Psychology: Science and Practice, 2, 144–156. https://doi.org/10.1093/clipsy.bpg016

Consider an example of yourself driving a car. You need to be fully conscious and aware of the present moment to drive out on the roads. Any minimal distraction can become a life-threatening accident, so you must maintain concentration and be aware of your surroundings and conditions to avoid collision. Even if you get distracted, you force your mind to return to the present and take hold of the situation.

Similarly, your life is that highway on which you are driving. If you are unaware of the present and stuck in the past or the future, you will miss out on the significant details that warn you of an incoming danger. To keep your focus rooted in the present, you must be mindful of the current moment and stop your thoughts from deviating unnecessarily.

Impact of Mindfulness on the Brain

"The present moment is a precious gift, and mindfulness helps us appreciate and enjoy it more fully."

-Sharon Salzberg

Several researches conducted on mindfulness have shown that it has positive impacts on the brain. It is a tool for changing your mindset and an effective practice to achieve harmony and balance in your life by getting in tune with the present moment.

Some of the positive impacts shown through research are discussed below:

1.   **Increases gray matter:** The gray matter in our brain consists of a large number of neurons that enable it to control the central nervous system. Its main function is to enable humans to control movement, memory, and emotions. Research has found that mindfulness meditation can increase the density of gray matter in the brain, particularly in areas associated with attention, emotional regulation, and self-awareness. Thus, if you use mindfulness, you can establish better control over your mind and body.[22]

2.   **Changes in brain function:** Mindfulness has been shown to activate certain areas of the brain associated with attention and emotional regulation while reducing activity in areas associated with mind wandering and self-referential thinking. The brain function improves once it is freed of all the clutter from thoughts about the past and the future. Focusing only on the present enables it to work better and take control of the surroundings, thus enabling you to be more aware of the things happening around you and impacting you currently.[23]

---

[22] Hölzel, B. K., Carmody, J., Vangel, M., Congleton, C., Yerramsetti, S. M., Gard, T., & Lazar, S. W. (2011). Mindfulness practice leads to increases in regional brain gray matter density. Psychiatry Research: Neuroimaging, 1, 36–43. https://doi.org/10.1016/j.pscychresns.2010.08.006

[23] Hasenkamp, W., & Barsalou, L. W. (2012). Effects of Meditation Experience on Functional Connectivity of Distributed Brain Networks. Frontiers in Human Neuroscience. https://doi.org/10.3389/fnhum.2012.00038

3. **Improves connectivity:** Mindfulness has been found to increase connectivity between different regions of the brain. Due to better connectivity, the brain is empowered to process and make decisions more accurately. You can also avoid brain fatigue through mindfulness, which boosts your brain to work at its optimum level.[24]

4. **Reduces stress:** Mindfulness has been shown to reduce activity in the amygdala, a brain region involved in the stress response, and increase activity in the prefrontal cortex, which is associated with executive function and emotional regulation. Taking a moment to think and remind yourself of the present puts your decisions in perspective and helps you choose the right approach. Thus, you no longer have to stress about making the wrong choices and suffering consequences.[25]

Tips to Practice Mindfulness Daily

You can only benefit from mindfulness if you make it a habit. Practicing it for a few hours and then going back to your stressful multitasking routine will deprive you of reaping its benefits. You have to commit to it, but don't worry, as it is not difficult to manage at all. You just have to start making slow

---

[24] Tang, Y.-Y., Lu, Q., Fan, M., Yang, Y., & Posner, M. I. (2012). Mechanisms of white matter changes induced by meditation. Proceedings of the National Academy of Sciences, 26, 10570–10574. https://doi.org/10.1073/pnas.1207817109

[25] Creswell, J. D. (2017). Mindfulness Interventions. Annual Review of Psychology, 1, 491–516. https://doi.org/10.1146/annurev-psych-042716-051139

but steady changes to your routine, and eventually, you will be able to incorporate mindfulness into your life completely.

Some mindfulness tips for everyday living are discussed below:

1. **Take a few deep breaths:** The easiest tip to practice mindfulness is deep breathing. When you feel stressed or overwhelmed, taking a few deep breaths can help to calm your mind and body. Focus on your breath as you inhale and exhale, and try to slow your breathing down. Incorporate it into your daily life as you can practice it anywhere with ease' just allot a few minutes to deep breathing every hour or two. You will start noticing the positive difference it creates in your mental well-being in a very short time.[26]

2. **Pay attention to your senses:** Take a moment to notice what you can see, hear, smell, taste, and touch. The sensory details of your surroundings help you to root them in your mind, creating conscious memories. Once you start paying attention to the details, your mind will not deviate to the past or the future. Instead, it will help to bring you into the present moment and increase your awareness.[27]

------

[26] Harvard Health Publishing. (2018). Relaxation techniques: Breath control helps quell errant stress response. Retrieved from https://www.health.harvard.edu/mind-and-mood/relaxation-techniques-breath-control-helps-quell-errant-stress-response

[27] Greater Good Science Center at UC Berkeley. (n.d.). Mindfulness. Retrieved from https://ggsc.berkeley.edu/what_we_do/mindfulness

3. **Practice gratitude:** Another helpful tip is to list down all the things in your life that are important to you and make life easier. Take time each day to reflect on the things you are grateful for, such as your family, friends, pets, car, or other necessities that you end up taking for granted. This can help cultivate positive emotions and increase happiness while making you feel that you are living contentedly.[28]

4. **Take breaks from technology:** In this rapid world of technology and gadgets, most of us find it impossible to live without our smartphones. However, the increased screen time and the variety of options you get to explore on the phone make your brain tired without even realizing it. It affects your mental as well as physical health by making you lethargic, affecting your eyesight, decreasing your concentration, and lowering your productivity. Try to disconnect from your phone and other devices for periods of time each day. This can help to reduce stress, improve your health, and increase mindfulness.[29]

5. **Practice mindful eating:** Take time to savor and enjoy your food, paying attention to the tastes, textures, and smells. Incorporate all your five senses in the act of eating your food

[28] Emmons, R. A., & McCullough, M. E. (2003). Counting blessings versus burdens: An experimental investigation of gratitude and subjective well-being in daily life. Journal of Personality and Social Psychology, 2, 377–389. https://doi.org/10.1037/0022-3514.84.2.377

[29] Tandoc, E. C., Ferrucci, P., & Duffy, M. (2015). Facebook use, envy, and depression among college students: Is facebooking depressing? Computers in Human Behavior, 139–146. https://doi.org/10.1016/j.chb.2014.10.053

and be mindful of what it is, where it came from, and how it got to the table. In this way, you will be grateful for the food and concentrate fully on eating it instead of being distracted by television, phones, or random conversations. This technique can help to increase your awareness and improve digestion.[30]

The Mindful S.N.A.C.K.[31]

The Mindful S.N.A.C.K. is a simple mindfulness exercise that can be used to promote mindful eating. This practice can help increase your awareness and enjoyment of food while promoting healthy eating habits.

The acronym S.N.A.C.K. stands for Stop, Notice, Accept, Curiosity, and Kindness. Here's a breakdown of each step:

1. **Stop:** Pause before you start eating and take a moment to breathe deeply and relax.

2. **Notice:** Pay attention to the colors, textures, and smells of your food, as well as the sensations in your body as you eat.

---

[30] Albers, S. (2017). Mindful Eating: A Guide to Rediscovering a Healthy and Joyful Relationship with Food. New Harbinger Publications.
[31] Naumburg, C. (2016, November 18). How to Take a Mindful S.N.A.C.K. Moment - Mindful. Mindful. https://www.mindful.org/how-to-take-mindful-snack/

3. **Accept:** Allow yourself to fully experience the taste of the food without judging or criticizing it.

4. **Curiosity:** Be curious about the food and how it affects your body and mind.

5. **Kindness:** Be kind to yourself as you eat, and avoid criticizing or judging yourself for what you are eating.

Conclusion

Mindfulness helps you recenter on the present moment, bringing awareness to the *now*. This is difficult as your mind/ego wants you to be rooted in the past (stressing over failures) or the future (giving anxiety over the unknown).

Consider how small changes have a big impact over time, as we saw with the turtle in the race. He proceeded confidently and mindfully advanced forward until he reached the finish line. Meanwhile, the rabbit was scatterbrained and unsure where he would land on each step as he bounced around and got distracted. All that overthinking exhausted him and drove him off course, resulting in him losing the race. Thus, the turtle's mindset was the real reason he won the race.

To change your mindset, you have to bring mindfulness into your life as a crucial element. Focus on one thing, such as eating, and when your mind wanders, remind it to come back to the present moment and stay on course. Practicing this technique will free your brain of all the clutter and improve your mental and physical well-being.

Remember, your ego doesn't deal with the real, present moments. It only replays the past movie to you on how you previously did or a trailer of what it thinks you will do. Don't forget that you can change the movie script.

You're alive, can think, and have meaning and purpose for your actions. So, take charge of your life and be mindful of every passing moment instead of staying rooted in thoughts of the past or the future.

Only you can make a positive difference for yourself, so don't miss out on this golden opportunity to transform your life by incorporating the practice of mindfulness.

Chapter 7: Meditation

"Meditation is not a means of escape from the world but a way to come into contact with it."

-Thich Nhat Hanh

You would often see the words *mindfulness* and *meditation* together; sometimes, people use them interchangeably. However, both these terms are different, and the only reason people get confused is that they are targeting a similar goal.

Mindfulness and meditation both enable you to be more aware of yourself and improve your mental well-being. The key difference is that mindfulness is a state, while meditation is a technique used to reach that state.

Coming back to the tale of the turtle and the rabbit, we see that the turtle is mindful of his present situation, but how did he achieve it? He was able to do so through meditation. He paused to think, created space in the prefrontal cortex of his brain, and meditated to reach the best response for his present situation.

Similarly, we can reap the benefits of the turtle mindset if we incorporate meditation into our busy routines. Through meditation, we can connect to our inner self, be more conscious of our surroundings, and reduce the stress of our lives by dedicating some time to relax and unwind.

In this chapter, we will discuss meditation, how it impacts the brain, and the benefits it has on your mental health. We will also discuss a few simple ways to practice meditation regularly.

What Is Meditation?

Meditation is a mental practice and an exercise of consciousness, allowing you to reach a focused state of mind by being aware of your present and conscious of your thoughts, feelings, and emotions.

It has been practiced for thousands of years in several cultures to promote spirituality and wellness. However, the origin of meditation can be traced back to ancient Vedic times in India. Meditation is one of the modalities described in Ayurveda (The Science of Life). According to Ancient Vedic texts, the true purpose of meditation is to connect oneself to the deep inner self.[32]

Nowadays, meditation comprises diverse activities such as conscious breathing, yoga, tai chi, and observing mantras to achieve a focused state of mind. Different apps, books, music, and guided videos have made it very easy for people to practice meditation. With a single touch of your phone or laptop, you can find multiple resources on meditation techniques and how to incorporate them into your routine. So,

---

[32] Sharma, H. (2015). Meditation: Process and effects. AYU (An International Quarterly Journal of Research in Ayurveda), 3, 233. https://doi.org/10.4103/0974-8520.182756

you don't need to take out a lot of time from your day to practice meditation.

The first thing you need to know about meditation is that there is no wrong approach. However, you must practice it regularly if you want to experience the positive difference it can create in your life. Whether you meditate for three minutes or three hours per day, if you do it regularly, you will reap the benefits, and there is no need to be competitive about it. It all depends on what suits you best and what technique you can follow easily.

For example, you start meditating by focusing on an apple on the table before you. Take a deep breath, empty your mind of all thoughts, and bring your focus to the apple. If your mind drifts off to some other thought, and it will happen and is very normal, then you must bring your thoughts back to the apple.

Don't follow that thought process somewhere else like the rabbit did when getting distracted from the race. Instead, root yourself in the present and put all your focus on the apple, just like the turtle focuses solely on reaching the finish line. It is a simple exercise, but it will help you train your mind to focus on what matters and not deviate.

If you fall asleep while practicing meditation, there is no need to fret about it, as perhaps that is what your body needs at that moment. While meditating, you are training yourself to be aware of yourself and your needs, so if sleep overcomes you, your body needs that time to relax.

Practicing Meditation

"Meditation is not a way of making your mind quiet. It's a way of entering into the quiet that's already there—buried under the 50,000 thoughts the average person thinks every day."

-Deepak Chopra

There are various forms of meditation practice, including both physical and mental exercises. The most common is the conscious breathing method, in which you meditate by focusing on your breathing and consciously regulating it. Some people prefer meditating through yoga as it engages all the parts of their body. Others prefer going on meditative walks or enhancing their self-consciousness through the repetition of positive statements.

Here is an example of a basic meditation exercise:

- Find a comfortable seat in a quiet, peaceful environment where you will not be disturbed. You can sit on a cushion on the floor or in a chair, whichever is most comfortable for you.

- Set a timer for your desired length of meditation. Start with a shorter period of time, such as 5-10 minutes, and gradually increase as you become more comfortable with the practice.

- Close your eyes and take a few deep breaths, allowing your body to relax and settle.

- Bring your attention to the present moment by focusing on your breath. Notice the sensation of the breath as it enters and exits your body. You can focus on the rise and fall of your chest or the sensation of air entering and escaping your lungs.

- If your mind begins to wander, simply notice the thoughts or distractions that arise without judgment or criticism. Then, gently bring your attention back to your breath.

- Continue to focus on your breath, bringing your attention back each time your mind wanders. You may also choose to expand your awareness to other sensations in your body or the environment around you, but try to remain focused on the present moment.

- When the timer goes off, take a few deep breaths and allow your body to settle before opening your eyes.

Remember that meditation is a practice that takes time and patience to develop. It is not a competition as every mind and body responds to it in its own way. But the more you practice it, the better results you will reap. With regular practice, you can cultivate greater awareness, calm, and well-being in your life.

Effects of Meditation

Scientific research has shown that regular meditation practice can have numerous benefits for mental and physical health, including reducing symptoms of anxiety and depression, improving cognitive function, and enhancing immune function.[33]

The effects of meditation are closely linked to its process. It doesn't matter what exercise or practice you choose, but doing it regularly changes your brain function. This is also explained through neuroplasticity, where conscious breathing and mindfulness can change your brain's response from immediate and reactive to thoughtful and positive.

Some of the common effects experienced by people who meditate regularly are discussed below:

1. Reduced activity in the amygdala: During meditation, you are letting go of all the clutter from your life and focusing only on the thoughts and feelings in the present moment. Thus, your brain will not overthink and neither deviate to unnecessary thoughts that can induce stress. Meditation also reduces activity in the amygdala, a brain region involved in the stress response. It increases activity in the prefrontal cortex,

---

[33] Goyal, M., Singh, S., Sibinga, E. M. S., Gould, N. F., Rowland-Seymour, A., Sharma, R., Berger, Z., Sleicher, D., Maron, D. D., Shihab, H. M., Ranasinghe, P. D., Linn, S., Saha, S., Bass, E. B., & Haythornthwaite, J. A. (2014). Meditation Programs for Psychological Stress and Well-being. JAMA Internal Medicine, 3, 357.
https://doi.org/10.1001/jamainternmed.2013.13018

associated with executive function and emotional regulation. As a result, when you meditate, your mind gets trained to respond positively, which reduces your stress levels.[34]

2. Increased energy and performance: As accumulated stresses are removed, your energy increases, and you will be more capable of dealing with daily tasks. It boosts your performance and increases efficiency.

3. Better memory: People who meditate have better memory as they are constantly regulating their nervous system and boosting their brain function. It has also been used as an essential tool for the prevention of Alzheimer's disease along with other modalities such as dietary modification, physical exercise, mental stimulation, and socialization.[35]

4. Physiological benefits: Meditation also has several physiological benefits, such as reduced blood pressure, regulated heart rate, reduced cholesterol, and increased regional cerebral blood flow.[36]

---

[34] Creswell, J. D. (2017). Mindfulness Interventions. Annual Review of Psychology, 1, 491–516. https://doi.org/10.1146/annurev-psych-042716-051139

[35] Khalsa, D. S. (2015). Stress, Meditation, and Alzheimer's Disease Prevention: Where The Evidence Stands. Journal of Alzheimer's Disease, 1, 1–12. https://doi.org/10.3233/jad-142766

[36] Horowitz, S. (2010). Health Benefits of Meditation: What the Newest Research Shows. Alternative and Complementary Therapies, 4, 223–228. https://doi.org/10.1089/act.2010.16402

All these benefits and more can be observed when you meditate regularly and let the practice become an essential part of your life.

Brain's Response to Meditation

During meditation, the brain undergoes changes in connectivity and activity, which can reduce stress and increase relaxation. The prefrontal cortex of the brain can be strengthened through meditation. As it is the region responsible for decision-making, meditation helps it to be active and respond promptly to every situation.[37]

Furthermore, while you meditate, you train your body to switch from the sympathetic nervous system (SNS) to the parasympathetic nervous system (PNS). When you train yourself to shift from the SNS to the PNS state, you shift from a flight or fight response to a rest and relax response. Instead of reacting immediately to a situation, you are taking your time to respond in the best possible way.

Just like the turtle who meditated and then responded to the decision to use the lake to cover the distance, you will also respond to the situation instead of giving an instant reaction that might not be so favorable in the long run.

---

[37] Hölzel, B. K., Carmody, J., Vangel, M., Congleton, C., Yerramsetti, S. M., Gard, T., & Lazar, S. W. (2011). Mindfulness practice leads to increases in regional brain gray matter density. Psychiatry Research: Neuroimaging, 1, 36–43. https://doi.org/10.1016/j.pscychresns.2010.08.006

Listed below are some responses of the brain to meditation, recorded and proven in scientific research:

1.   Changes in brain waves: Different types of meditation can produce different patterns of brain waves, such as alpha waves (associated with relaxation) and theta waves (associated with deep meditation).[38]

2.   Changes in the prefrontal cortex: Studies have shown that regular meditation practice can increase the volume of gray matter in the prefrontal cortex, which is involved in attention, emotional regulation, and self-awareness. As you meditate, your brain responds positively to the process, and this increased gray matter helps you achieve a focused state of mind.[39]

3.   Decreased activity in the default mode network: The default mode network is a group of brain regions active when the mind is at rest and associated with self-referential thinking and mind-wandering. When you are not doing anything important or in a resting state, you will find your attention wanders off to random thoughts. This is an effect of your brain going into the default mode.

---

[38] Chiesa, A., & Serretti, A. (2009). A systematic review of neurobiological and clinical features of mindfulness meditations. Psychological Medicine, 8, 1239–1252. https://doi.org/10.1017/s0033291709991747

[39] Tang, Y.-Y., Lu, Q., Fan, M., Yang, Y., & Posner, M. I. (2012). Mechanisms of white matter changes induced by meditation. Proceedings of the National Academy of Sciences, 26, 10570–10574. https://doi.org/10.1073/pnas.1207817109

During meditation, activity in the default mode network is reduced, allowing greater focus and attention on the present moment. Thus, the brain is able to return to its focused state with ease through regular meditation practices instead of getting distracted by aimless thoughts and losing track of your thinking while at rest.[40]

4.   Enhanced connectivity: Meditation has been shown to enhance connectivity between different brain regions, including those involved in attention, emotion regulation, and interception. It improves overall brain function and enhances response to immediate situations.[41]

The R.A.I.N Meditation by Tara Brach

Tara Brach, American psychologist and author, has written extensively on the R.A.I.N. meditation and has recorded guided meditations that walk you through the practice. Her technique, the R.A.I.N. meditation, is also featured in her book

---

[40] Brewer, J. A., Worhunsky, P. D., Gray, J. R., Tang, Y.-Y., Weber, J., & Kober, H. (2011). Meditation experience is associated with differences in default mode network activity and connectivity. Proceedings of the National Academy of Sciences, 50, 20254–20259.
https://doi.org/10.1073/pnas.1112029108

[41] Fox, K. C. R., Nijeboer, S., Dixon, M. L., Floman, J. L., Ellamil, M., Rumak, S. P., Sedlmeier, P., & Christoff, K. (2014). Is meditation associated with altered brain structure? A systematic review and meta-analysis of morphometric neuroimaging in meditation practitioners. Neuroscience & Biobehavioral Reviews, 48–73.
https://doi.org/10.1016/j.neubiorev.2014.03.016

Radical Compassion: Learning to Love Yourself and Your World with the Practice of R.A.I.N.

R.A.I.N. is a mindfulness meditation practice with four easy steps that help you connect with your inner self and reach a higher level of consciousness.

A breakdown of each step is discussed below:

1.   Recognize: Start the meditation practice by recognizing and acknowledging whatever is present in your mind or body without judging or trying to change it.

2.   Allow: Allow the thoughts, feelings, or sensations to be present without trying to push them away or hold onto them. As you exist in the present moment, allow all the thoughts about it to seep in, but don't overthink in this state. Let them exist within you but not cause any hindrance to your calm.

3.   Investigate: Investigate these thoughts, feelings, or sensations with curiosity and compassion. This may involve asking questions such as "What is this?" or "What does this feel like in my body?"

4.   Nurture: Offer yourself kindness and compassion as you explore whatever is present within you, and allow yourself to feel any emotions that arise. This is the most important step as you are accepting yourself and embracing it in the present state.

R.A.I.N. is a very effective technique, and if you practice it regularly can help you develop mindfulness, compassion, and self-awareness. It can also be used to manage difficult emotions or challenging situations.

Conclusion

Meditation is a tool that encourages positive thinking and helps your brain to respond to situations rather than abruptly react to them. These exercises and regular practice not only give you physical health benefits but also improve your deeper spiritual connection, which positively impacts your mental wellness.

In short, it is a certain positive way of looking at things in the current moment, acknowledging them, and accepting them. For example, you must have heard the saying that there is no darkness, only an absence of light. Similarly, there is no hate, only an absence of love. To overcome that, you can train yourself to love and accept through meditation, and the best part is that it doesn't require a lot of effort on your part.

Take a few minutes out of your day to meditate through yoga, mala beads, or even conscious breathing. Acknowledge your existence in the present moment and make your mind aware of it. You don't have to do it for long periods, but make sure you meditate regularly, at least once daily. It will regulate your nervous system, help you feel calmer and more grateful, and boost your positivity about the things you feel and experience. Thus, it will become an essential part of your day when these few minutes of meditation will replace all the stress and fatigue with positivity and comfort.

You might not be able to see the effects immediately, but with time, you will notice a change in the way you respond, and people around you will also be able to point it out.

The key is to remain consistent, and if you can manage that, you will see for yourself the difference it will bring to your life, your overall health, and wellness.

Chapter 8: Start with Breathing

"Mindful breath is the love language of the nervous system. You communicate whether you want to calm, balance or boost your mindset/energy through different breath protocols and your nervous systems will always deliver accordingly. It's science."

-Sandy Abrams

Breathing is the most essential function of our body, and without it, we cannot survive. Every second of the day and night, we breathe, inhale oxygen, and release carbon dioxide without fail. According to experts, the average human adult takes 12 to 20 breaths per minute, which is up to 28,800 breaths per day.[42]

A person stops breathing only after death; otherwise, his body is trained to breathe in and out involuntarily. However, have you ever noticed that something we do without even keeping track of is, in fact, the most important function that keeps us alive?

Have you ever thought about how many times you inhale and exhale throughout the day? No, because to you, it is

---

[42] Chourpiliadis, C. (2022). Physiology, Respiratory Rate - StatPearls - NCBI Bookshelf. National Center for Biotechnology Information. https://www.ncbi.nlm.nih.gov/books/NBK537306/

something you do normally, without any prompting or external motivation.

The first thing you do when you come into this world is inhale; the last thing you will do upon leaving is exhale. Thus, breathing is essential and one of the few bodily functions that have occurred involuntarily since birth.

It happens just like the beating of our hearts. Even if we are not keeping track of it, the function takes place and, as a result, keeps us alive.

Most of the common meditation exercises and techniques involve breathing because it is a vital function. Through just a simple inhale and exhale, you can regulate your mood, release stress, and calm yourself down.

Breathing plays a pivotal role in our lives, and through this chapter, we will discuss how breathing consciously can impact our minds and bodies. The tips and tricks to practice conscious breathing and the benefits gained from it are all explained below.

What Is Conscious Breathing?

Conscious breathing is the act of developing an awareness of your breathing patterns and regulating the air as it moves in and out of your body. This practice is used as a meditation technique as well as a way to ensure focus. It is also known as deep breathing or mindful breathing.[43]

In simple words, conscious breathing is to put some thought into a process you do automatically and then reflect on how it makes you feel. You breathe without even realizing how many breaths you take, but if you focus on this process, take each breath in, and release it mindfully, you start responding rather than reacting. You are aware of your breaths and create space in the prefrontal cortex, boosting the brain's power to make good decisions.

This mindful awareness cultivated through conscious breathing is key to achieving the kind of focus and control that led the turtle to victory in his race against the rabbit.

The race between the turtle and the rabbit not only showed their opposite mindsets but also focused on the use of conscious breathing to achieve mindfulness. During the race, the rabbit was focused only on reaching the finish line and chose to sprint over to the end as fast as possible. His breaths were irregulated; he was hopping fast, and his body tired out easily as compared to the turtle.

Therefore, the rabbit had to stop and take a nap to rejuvenate himself, whereas the turtle reserved his energy from the start and steadily edged toward his goal. Each step he

---

[43] Hoshaw, C. (2022). Conscious Breathing: Benefits, Types, How to Practice, Safety. Healthline; Healthline Media.
https://www.healthline.com/health/mind-body/conscious-breathing

took toward the finish line was as regulated as each conscious breath he was taking. Thus, the turtle responded rather than reacted to his circumstances, eventually gaining victory over an animal much faster than him.

Practicing Conscious Breathing

"As the breath moves, so does the mind, and the mind ceases to move as the breath is stopped."

-Hatha Yoga Pradipika

Practicing conscious breathing is quite easy as you simply have to focus on your breathing pattern: inhale, hold it for a few seconds, and then exhale. The most common way to start conscious breathing is by imagining a balloon inside your stomach that fills up as you inhale and then releases all the air as you exhale.

Several smartphone apps are also designed to help promote conscious breathing and use it as a meditation exercise. Whether you are getting ready for a fitness workout, a yoga session, or a regular walk through the park, these apps will remind you to regulate your breathing first and then start with the exercise.

During transitions, the best time of the day is to practice conscious breathing easily and effectively. Waiting for a bus, going to work, returning from work, waiting for food, and all these transitions in which you switch from one role to the other, you can focus on your breathing and use any of the techniques above to make your transition mindful.

The several techniques to practice conscious breathing are discussed below:

1. Number Technique: For this breathing technique, you have to select a sequence of numbers and regulate your breath according to it. For example, if I chose sequences 4, 5, and 6, I have to inhale for 4 seconds, hold my breath for 5 seconds, and then exhale for 6 seconds. You can try with shorter sequences at first, such as 2, 3, and 4, then slowly increase the time according to your ease.

2. Box Breathing: Somewhat similar to the number technique, box breathing also focuses on a sequence, but the numbers in this sequence have to be the same unit. For example, if I inhale for four seconds, hold my breath for the same time, and then exhale for four seconds, I am practicing box breathing.

3. Nostril Breathing: Another exercise is to breathe through one of your nostrils while covering the other. In this technique, you put your thumb on one nostril and the index finger of the same hand on your forehead. You inhale through one nostril, hold it, and then exhale. Hold your breath again and bring your index finger on the other nostril and your thumb on the forehead. Then, you repeat the process.

4. Diaphragm Breathing: This is also known as breathing through your stomach. You put one hand on your chest and the other on your stomach. Then, you inhale through your nose, allowing your abdomen to rise and expand. You slowly exhale, gradually releasing the air you were holding in. Repeat the process for as long as you feel convenient.

Whether it takes you five minutes or twenty minutes in the transition state, you can practice conscious breathing easily and bring yourself to a state of mindful meditation. It is no doubt the easiest meditation exercise.

Benefits of Conscious Breathing

Conscious breathing is a simple but powerful tool that can have numerous benefits for both physical and mental health. Slowing down your breathing and being mindful of it can cause psycho-physiological changes in brain-body interaction. [44]

The multiple benefits of conscious breathing are discussed below:

1.   **Reduces anxiety:** Conscious breathing can activate the parasympathetic nervous system, which helps to counteract the "fight or flight" response that occurs during times of stress. Once you switch from the sympathetic nervous system to the parasympathetic, it improves your body's

---

[44] Zaccaro, A., Piarulli, A., Laurino, M., Garbella, E., Menicucci, D., Neri, B., & Gemignani, A. (2018). How Breath-Control Can Change Your Life: A Systematic Review on Psycho-Physiological Correlates of Slow Breathing. Frontiers in Human Neuroscience.
https://doi.org/10.3389/fnhum.2018.00353

response to external stimuli and increases the efficiency of autonomic functions. This can lead to feelings of relaxation and calmness and a reduction in stress and anxiety.[45]

2.   Improves concentration and focus: As the oxygen flow to the brain increases through conscious breathing, cognitive functions also improve considerably. This exercise enhances concentration and focus as you are regularly training yourself to hold in and let go of your breath for a fixed sequence.[46]

3.   Increases vitality: Conscious breathing can help increase oxygenation of the body, which can boost energy levels and promote feelings of vitality. When you start feeling tired during work, practice conscious breathing to refresh yourself and focus on your tasks effectively.

4.   Improves sleep: Regulating your breathing patterns through conscious breathing helps calm the mind and promote relaxation, which can lead to improved sleep quality and quantity. A healthy sleep pattern equals a healthy lifestyle, which you can achieve by breathing consciously.

---

[45] Pal, G. K., & Velkumary, S. (2004). Effect of short-term practice of breathing exercises on autonomic functions in normal human volunteers. Indian Journal of Medical Research.
https://pubmed.ncbi.nlm.nih.gov/15347862/

[46] Zanesco, A. P., & King, B. G. (2019). Slow breathing and the contemplative life: A neurophenomenological perspective. Annals of the New York Academy of Sciences, 1447(1), 29–43.

5. **Improves immunity:** Conscious breathing can help to reduce physical tension and pain by releasing muscular tension. The immune function of the body is also improved by reducing stress and promoting relaxation, enhancing the body's ability to fight off illness.

6. Reduces symptoms of anxiety and depression: This breathing practice can help to reduce symptoms of anxiety and depression. It also improves mood and overall well-being, enabling you to face life with a positive approach without getting stressed out immediately.[47]

Conclusion

Every journey starts with a single step, and in the journey to mindfulness, conscious breathing is an excellent starting point. You can practice it anywhere, anytime, and for as long as you like without needing any specific equipment.

Start with breathing and see how it transforms your life with every passing day. You will feel energized, your focus and concentration will improve, and your response to different situations will improve.

Every person wishes to be the best at their task without making any mistakes and making the right decisions for

---

[47] Jerath, R., Crawford, M. W., Barnes, V. A., & Harden, K. (2015). Self-Regulation of Breathing as a Primary Treatment for Anxiety. Applied Psychophysiology and Biofeedback, 2, 107–115. https://doi.org/10.1007/s10484-015-9279-8

problem-solving. Conscious breathing can help you unlock this potential. The constant chatter in your mind will be replaced by a sense of calm and control. You'll react less impulsively and with greater awareness, allowing you to navigate challenges with clarity and wisdom.

Remember, the journey to becoming the best version of yourself starts with a single breath. So, choose the technique that works best for you, practice it regularly, and get ready to embrace the best version of yourself.

"The breath is like an anchor in the present moment, and so whenever we notice that our mind has wandered, we can gently bring it back to the breath."

-Tara Brach

Chapter 9: Conclusion

"Now, this is not the end. It is not even the beginning of the end. But it is, perhaps, the end of the beginning."

-Winston Churchill

If the rabbit were a person, he would likely be characterized as confident, energetic, and capable but also overconfident, complacent, and prone to underestimating others. He might be someone who relies on his natural talents and quick abilities, often taking his success for granted and assuming that effort isn't necessary to achieve his goals. His tendency to procrastinate and take things easy could be seen in a laid-back attitude, often leading to last-minute scrambles when he realizes he's falling behind. Despite his abilities, his lack of consistent effort and underestimation of others' determination could lead to unexpected failures and missed opportunities.

If the turtle were a person, he would likely be characterized by the following traits:

1. Persistent: The turtle shows a steady, unwavering determination to reach his goals, regardless of obstacles or the speed at which he progresses.

2. Patient: He understands that success takes time and is willing to invest the necessary effort without rushing.

3. Humble: Unlike the rabbit, the turtle doesn't boast about his abilities. Instead, he quietly works towards his goals.

4. Reliable: People can count on the turtle to keep going, no matter how tough the journey gets.

5. Focused: He keeps his eyes on the finish line, not getting distracted by others or by immediate gratification.

6. Resilient: The turtle doesn't get discouraged easily. He continues to move forward, even if the progress seems slow.

These characteristics enable the turtle to achieve success through consistent effort and resilience.

The following tables demonstrate a clear comparison between the turtle and the rabbit, their dominant traits, and the benefits of meditative practices on them:

Trait	Turtle	Rabbit
Speed	Slow and steady	Fast and quick
Persistence	Highly persistent	Lacks persistence
Patience	Very patient	Impatient
Confidence	Humble and self-assured	Overconfident

Focus	Consistently focused	Easily distracted
Attitude	Humble and hardworking	Boastful and complacent
Reliability	Reliable and dependable	Unreliable and inconsistent
Resilience	Resilient and determined	Easily discouraged if faced with failure
Approach	Methodical and careful	Careless and assumes success
Response to Challenges	Keeps moving forward regardless of difficulties	Overestimates abilities and underestimates challenges

Practice	Benefits for the Turtle	Benefits for the Rabbit
Mindfulness	Enhanced focus and concentration Stress reduction Increased resilience	Improved patience Better focus and attention Reduced overconfidence Emotional regulation

Meditation	Deepened focus and concentration. Further stress reduction. Increased patience and perseverance	Enhanced self-awareness Improved patience Better focus and attention Balanced confidence
Conscious Breathing	Enhanced focus and concentration Stress reduction Increased resilience	Improved patience Better focus and attention Emotional regulation Balanced confidence

What the Turtle Learns from the Rabbit

1. Embracing Speed: The turtle can learn the value of moving more quickly when appropriate, understanding that there are times when faster progress can be beneficial.

2. Confidence: The turtle can adopt a bit of the rabbit's confidence, realizing that self-assurance can enhance performance when balanced with humility.

3. Taking Breaks: Observing the rabbit, the turtle can understand that short, well-timed breaks can prevent burnout and rejuvenate energy for better overall performance.

What the Rabbit Learns from the Turtle

1. Patience and Persistence: The rabbit can learn the importance of being patient and persistent, understanding that consistent effort often leads to long-term success.

2. Humility: The rabbit can see the value in being humble and not underestimating others, recognizing that arrogance can lead to complacency and failure.

3. Focus and Steadiness: The rabbit can appreciate the importance of maintaining a steady focus on goals rather than getting distracted or overly confident in his abilities.

Can the Two Work Together?

Yes, the turtle and the rabbit can work together effectively by combining their strengths and compensating for each other's weaknesses. Here's how:

1. Complementary Skills: The turtle's persistence and patience can balance the rabbit's speed and confidence, creating a well-rounded team.

2. Mutual Learning: Working together allows both to learn from each other, improving their individual weaknesses while enhancing their strengths.

3. Strategic Planning: They can strategize together, with the rabbit handling tasks that require quick action and the turtle managing long-term, steady progress.

4. Mutual Support: The rabbit can motivate the turtle during slower phases, while the turtle can remind the rabbit to stay focused and not rush unnecessarily.

5. Balanced Approach: Together, they can achieve a balanced approach, where the rabbit's quick thinking and the turtle's careful planning ensure thorough and efficient progress.

Example of Working Together

Project Management — In a project, the rabbit could tackle immediate, short-term tasks requiring fast action, while the turtle focuses on long-term goals and ensures consistent progress. Their combined efforts would ensure that the project moves forward quickly yet steadily, with both immediate and future goals being met efficiently.

In conclusion, by learning from each other and working together, the turtle and the rabbit can create a synergistic partnership that leverages the best of both worlds, leading to greater success than either could achieve alone.

If we consider the turtle and rabbit as metaphors for different approaches to life and thought patterns, their impact on the brain and mind would manifest in several ways:

Turtle (Steady and Persistent Approach)

1. Brain Structure: The turtle's approach, characterized by steady perseverance and patience, may lead to structural changes in the brain associated with resilience and long-term planning. This could include strengthened connections in the prefrontal cortex, which is involved in decision-making and goal-setting.

2. Mindfulness and Focus: Living like a turtle would likely promote mindfulness practices and enhance focus. This could lead to increased gray matter density in areas associated with attention and emotional regulation, such as the anterior cingulate cortex and hippocampus.

3. Emotional Regulation: The turtle's steady pace and persistence would support emotional regulation, potentially reducing the size and activity of the amygdala, which is involved in processing emotions like fear and stress.

4. Learning and Memory: The turtle's methodical approach to life may enhance learning and memory consolidation processes, possibly leading to improvements in hippocampal function and neuroplasticity.

Rabbit (Quick and Impulsive Approach)

1. Brain Activation: The rabbit's quick and impulsive nature may result in heightened activity in regions of the brain associated with reward and instant gratification, such as the nucleus accumbens and ventral tegmental area.

2. Dopamine Release: Rapid decision-making and seeking of rewards may lead to frequent dopamine releases, reinforcing behaviors associated with immediate outcomes and pleasure.

3. Risk-Taking Behavior: The rabbit's tendency towards risk-taking and speed may influence brain areas involved in assessing risks and rewards, potentially altering the balance between impulsivity and caution.

4. Stress Response: The rabbit's lifestyle may contribute to heightened stress responses and cortisol levels, impacting areas of the brain like the hypothalamus and hippocampus, which regulate stress hormones and memory.

Integration and Impact

Balanced Living: Integrating aspects of both the turtle and rabbit approaches can lead to a balanced lifestyle. This might involve leveraging the rabbit's quick decision-making in situations requiring agility while adopting the turtle's patience and persistence for long-term goals.

Neuroplasticity: The brain's ability to change and adapt (neuroplasticity) means that individuals can develop habits and thought patterns that combine the strengths of both approaches. Regular practice of mindfulness, conscious decision-making, and reflection can enhance neuroplasticity and support a balanced brain function.

Mindfulness Practices: Both the turtle and rabbit can benefit from mindfulness practices, which promote awareness of thoughts and behaviors. This can lead to more deliberate decision-making and a better balance between immediate gratification and long-term success.

In essence, living through the examples of the turtle and rabbit can impact the brain and mind by shaping neural pathways, influencing emotional responses, and enhancing cognitive functions.

Adopting a balanced approach that integrates the strengths of both characters can lead to a more resilient, focused, and emotionally regulated way of engaging with life.

The Final Note

Here's to starting a new journey of awareness in mindful living. I conclude the tale of the rabbit and the turtle by stating that their victory or defeat in the race was not the end of their journey. Instead, it was the beginning of a lifelong process of learning their strengths and weaknesses together.

The rabbit learned from the turtle, and the turtle also continued to seek improvement. Just like you—the readers— have learned from this book and hope to apply the findings in your daily lives.

As we studied the mindset of the rabbit and the turtle, many of you would think that the turtle mindset is better as it helps us respond rather than react. However, the truth is that we must achieve a balance between the turtle and the rabbit mindset to be successful in life.

In some instances, an immediate reaction is necessary, but you don't have enough time to think. If you follow the turtle mindset, you might fail, as it would take all of your time. Therefore, we should minimize the rabbit mindset in our lives but not neglect it altogether, as it is applicable in situations where we need to come to a conclusion quickly. Both mindsets have advantages and disadvantages; how and when we utilize them is more critical to success.

Life, in general, is a learning process, and no certified manual exists on how you should lead your life. However, you can make positive changes to improve your experience by observing other people, learning from their wisdom, and seeing if it applies to you. Any change you bring to your life will be gradual, just like the differences you experience after regular meditation. You might not be able to point out these positive effects instantly, but others will notice their impact on your health, personality, and lifestyle.

Instead of being competitive in life, we should learn to be more collaborative. Be kind to yourself, and don't rush yourself into anything. Take a deep breath, relax, and create some space in the prefrontal cortex of your brain through conscious breathing. Then, analyze the situation and reap the benefits of responding to it effectively.

Forming good habits and breaking bad ones doesn't happen in a day. You have to accept the change, don't force yourself into it, allow time and flexibility, and slowly but steadily work on improving yourself. Therefore, being kind to yourself is very important, and you must understand that to bring a positive change in your life, you have to put in the effort.

It doesn't matter how big or small steps you took to reach the objective; what matters is that you were consistent and kept pacing ahead.

If you have been dealing with a complex situation for a long time, you cannot overcome it in a day. So don't pressurize yourself into working for immediate change. Start slow with small things of self-awareness, creating more space in your actions and responses, being more mindful, and having the ability to meditate and reflect.

Throughout this book, we discussed mindfulness meditation, its impact on individuals, and the techniques to incorporate it into our lives. The core concept of this book is to familiarize you with the different mindsets and how you can regulate them to make the most out of any challenge you face.

Being more mindful and aware of your surroundings helps you respond to them positively; being present in the current moment makes you appreciate the little things you could have ignored otherwise.

The key takeaways from this book are:

Finding Peace in the Present Moment

Even if you are stuck in a storm, you can find peace in the present moment by looking inward. When it feels like you're in chaos, do not fret. Take a moment to pause and reflect, then find the calm inside yourself. In this fast-paced world, everyone acts like a rabbit to quickly jump to conclusions and find solutions in less time.

But you must understand that taking a moment to find your center and then responding to the situation creates a big difference. We don't always have to react immediately; we can find the right time to respond. Ask yourself these three questions before responding:

Is there a need to respond to this?

Am I the one who has to respond?

And am I the one who has to respond to it right now?

Through these questions, you can prioritize your tasks, face the challenges you absolutely have to face, and save yourself from draining your energy and effort on tasks that do not specifically demand your response.

Personal Insights

Every person's experience is different, and we cannot find a single solution that fits all. Experiment and adapt the techniques that work for you, start slow but stay consistent, and make mindfulness meditation a lifelong practice. Our thoughts generate words and emotions, both of which are powerful things that we need to be more mindful of. Through conscious breathing, we can better understand what is happening around us and how we need to respond. Think about what you want to do each day in the morning, and then, at the end of the day, reflect on what you were able to accomplish. Keep in mind that failure is not the end of the journey. It is a small hiccup that you need to overcome and move ahead, equipped with the knowledge of how to avoid that failure again.

For me, this book is an expression of my journey of going through these positive changes created in my life through mindfulness meditation. It is an attempt to extend what I have learned through my mentors, such as Tara Brach, Dr. Rick Hansen, Eckhart Tolle, and Jack Kornfield. It is a compilation of these gradual changes that I could incorporate into my life under their guidance, and I wanted to share these learnings so that others can find it beneficial, too. Hopefully, the insights and learning from this book will enable you to create a positive difference in your life.

This, alone, was the main motivation for me to write this book.

Most of the battle is in our inner thoughts, as throughout the day, from the start to the end, we are thinking, and our brains are processing hundreds of thoughts at the same time. Sometimes, it feels like our brain is a runaway train with no direction. So, it is very important to slow this process down and realize that we are just observers of our thoughts; we are not the thoughts themselves.

Ultimately, I would reiterate that it is never too late to start. You can start meditation now and practice conscious breathing and other mindfulness techniques. It is never too late to do something better for yourself. Investing in yourself is not selfish; it is a healthy trait because a better you will eventually make a better us. Being truthful to yourself is most important; in the long term, the people around you will also respect and appreciate it.

This book is merely a guidepost. Now, it's your turn to take the wheel. Remember, mindful living starts with a single exhale, and with each conscious breath, you become the master of your own experience.

Embrace the journey and watch your life unfold with newfound clarity, focus, and inner peace.

Chapter 10: Weekly Meditation Plan

Below, you will find a three-week meditation plan taking you on a mindful journey through psychological and spiritual wellness. This plan is a kickstarter for you to dive into the vast world of meditation and reap its benefits.

Each day will bring forth new challenges and possibilities. It depends on how you turn them into opportunities for personal development.

After these three weeks, you can choose your daily meditation practices based on what exercise resonates with you most. Remember, you are on a journey where no competition exists regarding how long it takes to reach your destination, but what matters most is the process involved in fulfilling your objective.

So, without further ado, let's dive into this weekly meditation plan.

WEEK 1

MONDAY

Daily Meditation

Find a Quiet Space: Sit comfortably and close your eyes. Take a few deep breaths, inhaling deeply through your nose and exhaling slowly through your mouth. Allow your breath to return to its natural rhythm.

Mindful Breathing: Focus on your breath. Notice the sensation of the air entering and leaving your body. If your mind wanders, gently bring your focus back to your breath.

Gratitude Visualization: Think of three things you are grateful for today. Visualize each one clearly in your mind. Feel the gratitude filling your heart with warmth and positivity.

Mantra Meditation: Silently repeat a calming phrase or word, such as "peace" or "calm." Continue this for several minutes, allowing the word to anchor your mind. Include "I AM" with the mantra.

Closing: Slowly bring your awareness back to your surroundings. Take a few deep breaths and gently open your eyes. Carry this sense of peace with you throughout the day.

Daily Affirmation

"I am at peace with who I am and who I am becoming. I trust in the journey of life and embrace the possibilities of today with an open heart and mind."

TUESDAY

Daily Meditation

Find a Comfortable Position: Sit comfortably and close your eyes. Take a few deep breaths, inhaling deeply through your nose and exhaling slowly through your mouth. Allow your breath to return to its natural rhythm.

Body Scan: Slowly bring your attention to different parts of your body, starting from your toes and moving up to your head. Notice any sensations or tension and consciously relax each part.

Gratitude Reflection: Think of three people in your life for whom you are grateful today. Visualize each one clearly in your mind. Feel the gratitude filling your heart with warmth and positivity.

Mantra Meditation: Silently repeat a calming phrase or word, such as "love" or "joy." Continue this for several minutes, allowing the word to anchor your mind. Include "I AM" with the mantra.

Closing: Slowly bring your awareness back to your surroundings. Take a few deep breaths and gently open your eyes. Carry this sense of peace with you throughout the day.

Daily Affirmation

"I am grateful for the people in my life and the love that surrounds me. I open my heart to joy and kindness."

WEDNESDAY

Daily Meditation

Find a Quiet Space: Sit comfortably and close your eyes. Take a few deep breaths, inhaling deeply through your nose and exhaling slowly through your mouth. Allow your breath to return to its natural rhythm.

Mindful Breathing: Focus on your breath. Notice the sensation of the air entering and leaving your body. If your mind starts to wander, gently bring your focus back to your breath.

Gratitude Visualization: Think of three moments from the past week for which you are grateful. Visualize each one clearly in your mind. Feel the gratitude filling your heart with warmth and positivity.

Mantra Meditation: Silently repeat a calming phrase or word, such as "serenity" or "balance." Continue this for several minutes, allowing the word to anchor your mind. Include "I AM" with the mantra.

Closing: Slowly bring your awareness back to your surroundings. Take a few deep breaths and gently open your eyes. Carry this sense of peace with you throughout the day.

Daily Affirmation

"I am thankful for the moments of joy and growth. I embrace balance and serenity in my life."

THURSDAY

Daily Meditation

Find a Quiet Space: Sit comfortably and close your eyes. Take a few deep breaths, inhaling deeply through your nose and exhaling slowly through your mouth. Allow your breath to return to its natural rhythm.

Mindful Listening: Listen to the sounds around you without judgment. Notice the layers of sound and let them come and go, bringing your attention back to your breath if your mind wanders.

Gratitude Visualization: Think of three things in nature you are grateful for today. Visualize each one clearly in your mind. Feel the gratitude filling your heart with warmth and positivity.

Mantra Meditation: Silently repeat a calming phrase or word, such as "harmony" or "nature." Continue this for several minutes, allowing the word to anchor your mind. Include "I AM" with the mantra.

Closing: Slowly bring your awareness back to your surroundings. Take a few deep breaths and gently open your eyes. Carry this sense of peace with you throughout the day.

Daily Affirmation

"I am connected to the beauty and harmony of nature. I find peace and joy in the natural world."

FRIDAY

Daily Meditation

Find a Comfortable Position: Sit comfortably and close your eyes. Take a few deep breaths, inhaling deeply through your nose and exhaling slowly through your mouth. Allow your breath to return to its natural rhythm.

Body Awareness: Bring your attention to your feet. Notice how they feel and then move your awareness up through your legs, torso, arms, and head. Relax each part of your body as you go.

Gratitude Visualization: Think of three accomplishments from the past month for which you are grateful. Visualize each one clearly in your mind. Feel the gratitude filling your heart with warmth and positivity.

Mantra Meditation: Silently repeat a calming phrase or word, such as "strength" or "courage." Continue this for several minutes, allowing the word to anchor your mind. Include "I AM" with the mantra.

Closing: Slowly bring your awareness back to your surroundings. Take a few deep breaths and gently open your eyes. Carry this sense of peace with you throughout the day.

Daily Affirmation

"I am proud of my achievements and the progress I have made. I face challenges with strength and courage."

SATURDAY

Daily Meditation

Find a Quiet Space: Sit comfortably and close your eyes. Take a few deep breaths, inhaling deeply through your nose and exhaling slowly through your mouth. Allow your breath to return to its natural rhythm.

Mindful Visualization: Imagine a peaceful place like a beach or forest. Visualize it in detail, feeling the serenity and beauty of this place.

Gratitude Visualization: Think of three things you love about yourself. Visualize each one clearly in your mind. Feel the gratitude filling your heart with warmth and positivity.

Mantra Meditation: Silently repeat a calming phrase or word, such as "self-love" or "acceptance." Continue this for several minutes, allowing the word to anchor your mind.

Closing: Slowly bring your awareness back to your surroundings. Take a few deep breaths and gently open your eyes. Carry this sense of peace with you throughout the day.

Daily Affirmation

"I embrace and love myself completely. I am worthy of love and acceptance."

SUNDAY

Daily Meditation

Find a Comfortable Position: Sit comfortably and close your eyes. Take a few deep breaths, inhaling deeply through your nose and exhaling slowly through your mouth. Allow your breath to return to its natural rhythm.

Loving-Kindness Meditation: Focus on sending loving-kindness to yourself. Repeat phrases such as "May I be happy, may I be healthy, may I be at peace." Then, extend these wishes to others.

Gratitude Visualization: Think of three experiences from your life that brought you joy. Visualize each one clearly in your mind. Feel the gratitude filling your heart with warmth and positivity.

Mantra Meditation: Silently repeat a calming phrase or word, such as "joy" or "love." Continue this for several minutes, allowing the word to anchor your mind.

Closing: Slowly bring your awareness back to your surroundings. Take a few deep breaths and gently open your eyes. Carry this sense of peace with you throughout the day.

Daily Affirmation

"I am filled with joy and love. I share these feelings with the world around me."

WEEK 2

MONDAY

Gyan Mudra (Mudra of Knowledge)
How to Practice:

1. Sit comfortably with your spine straight.

2. Touch the tip of your index finger to the tip of your thumb.

3. Keep the other three fingers straight and relaxed.

4. Rest your hands on your knees with palms facing upwards.

5. Close your eyes and take deep breaths for 5-10 minutes.

Benefits: Enhances concentration and memory, promotes a calm and focused mind, and is believed to stimulate the root chakra, increasing mental stability.

GYAN MUDRA

TUESDAY

Prana Mudra (Mudra of Life)

How to Practice:

1. Sit comfortably with your spine straight.
2. Touch the tips of your little finger and ring finger to the tip of your thumb.
3. Keep the other two fingers straight.
4. Rest your hands on your knees with palms facing upwards.
5. Close your eyes and take deep breaths for 5-10 minutes.

Benefits: Boosts vitality, reduces fatigue, improves immune function, and enhances overall health and energy levels.

PRANA MUDRA

WEDNESDAY

Vayu Mudra (Mudra of Air)
How to Practice:

1. Sit comfortably with your spine straight.
2. Fold your index finger and press it with the base of your thumb.
3. Keep the other three fingers straight.
4. Rest your hands on your knees with palms facing upwards.
5. Close your eyes and take deep breaths for 5-10 minutes.

Benefits: Helps relieve rheumatic and arthritic pains, reduces anxiety and stress, and promotes a calm mind.

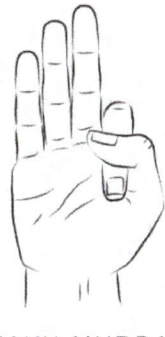

VAYU MUDRA

THURSDAY

Shunya Mudra (Mudra of Emptiness)
How to Practice:

1. Sit comfortably with your spine straight.
2. Fold your middle finger and press it with the base of your thumb.
3. Keep the other three fingers straight.
4. Rest your hands on your knees with palms facing upwards.
5. Close your eyes and take deep breaths for 5-10 minutes.

Benefits: Helps with ear and hearing issues, reduces numbness in the body, and balances the element of space within the body.

Shunya Mudra

FRIDAY

Surya Mudra (Mudra of the Sun)

How to Practice:

1. Sit comfortably with your spine straight.
2. Fold your ring finger and press it with the base of your thumb.
3. Keep the other three fingers straight.
4. Rest your hands on your knees with palms facing upwards.
5. Close your eyes and take deep breaths for 5-10 minutes.

Benefits: Enhances metabolism, aids in weight loss, improves digestion, and balances the boy's temperature.

SATURDAY

Varuna Mudra (Mudra of Water)
How to Practice:

1. Sit comfortably with your spine straight.
2. Touch the tip of your little finger to the tip of your thumb.
3. Keep the other three fingers straight.
4. Rest your hands on your knees with palms facing upwards.
5. Close your eyes and take deep breaths for 5-10 minutes.

Benefits: Helps retain water balance, improves skin health, and reduces dryness in the body.

Varun Mudra

SUNDAY

Dhyana Mudra (Mudra of Meditation)
How to Practice:

1. Sit comfortably with your spine straight.
2. Place your hands on your lap, your right hand on top of the left, and both palms facing upwards.
3. The tips of the thumbs gently touch each other, forming a triangle.
4. Close your eyes and take deep breaths for 5-10 minutes.

Benefits: Promotes deep meditation, enhances mental clarity and focus, and brings inner peace and tranquility.

Practicing these mudras daily can help in balancing physical, mental, and emotional health, bringing overall harmony and well-being.

Dhyana Mudra

WEEK 3

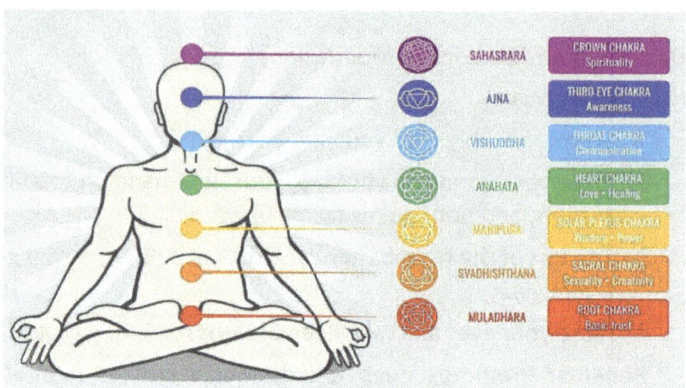

MONDAY

Root Chakra (Muladhara)

Location: Base of the spine

Color: Red

Element: Earth

Description: The Root Chakra, or Muladhara, is the foundation of our energy system. It represents our sense of security, stability, and grounding. This chakra is connected to our basic needs for survival, such as food, shelter, and safety. When balanced, it brings a sense of being grounded and secure. Imbalances may manifest as fear, anxiety, or financial instability.

> **Affirmation:**
>
> *"I am grounded, safe, and secure."*

TUESDAY

Sacral Chakra (Svadhisthana)

Location: Lower abdomen, about two inches below the navel

Color: Orange

Element: Water

Description: The Sacral Chakra, or Svadhisthana, governs our emotions, creativity, and sexual energy. It is the center of our passions, desires, and pleasure. A balanced Sacral Chakra fosters healthy relationships, creativity, and emotional well-being. Imbalances can lead to issues with emotional instability, creativity blocks, or sexual dysfunction.

Affirmation:

"I embrace my creativity and sensuality."

WEDNESDAY

Solar Plexus Chakra (Manipura)

Location: Upper abdomen, in the stomach area

Color: Yellow

Element: Fire

Description: The Solar Plexus Chakra, or Manipura, is the seat of our personal power, confidence, and self-esteem. It governs our ability to be in control of our lives and make decisions. When balanced, it enhances self-confidence, motivation, and a sense of purpose. Imbalances may result in low self-esteem, lack of direction, or control issues.

Affirmation:

"I am confident and in control of my life."

THURSDAY

Heart Chakra (Anahata)

Location: Center of the chest, just above the heart

Color: Green

Element: Air

Description: The Heart Chakra, or Anahata, is the center of love, compassion, and connection. It governs our ability to love and be loved, fostering relationships and emotional bonds. A balanced Heart Chakra promotes compassion, empathy, and emotional openness. Imbalances can manifest as jealousy, anger, or difficulty in relationships.

Affirmation:
"I am open to love and compassion."

FRIDAY

Throat Chakra (Vishuddha)
    Location: Throat
    Color: Blue
    Element: Ether (Space)
    Description: The Throat Chakra, or Vishuddha, is the center of communication and expression. It governs our ability to speak our truth, express our thoughts and feelings, and listen to others. A balanced Throat Chakra enhances clear communication and self-expression. Imbalances may result in difficulty expressing oneself, fear of speaking, or throat issues.

Affirmation:
    "I express myself clearly and confidently."

SATURDAY

Third Eye Chakra (Ajna)

Location: Forehead, between the eyebrows

Color: Indigo

Element: Light

Description: The Third Eye Chakra, or Ajna, is the center of intuition, insight, and wisdom. It governs our ability to see the bigger picture, access inner guidance, and develop a strong sense of intuition. A balanced Third Eye Chakra fosters clarity, insight, and spiritual awareness. Imbalances can lead to confusion, lack of focus, or disconnection from intuition.

Affirmation:
"I trust my intuition and inner wisdom."

SUNDAY

Crown Chakra (Sahasrara)

Location: Top of the head

Color: Violet or White

Element: Thought (Cosmic Energy)

Description: The Crown Chakra, or Sahasrara, is the highest chakra, representing our connection to the divine, spirituality, and higher consciousness. It governs our sense of enlightenment, unity, and spiritual connection. A balanced Crown Chakra brings a deep sense of peace, spiritual understanding, and connection to the universe. Imbalances can manifest as a sense of isolation, lack of purpose, or spiritual disconnect.

> **Affirmation:**
>
> *"I am connected to the divine and open to spiritual wisdom."*

Understanding and balancing these chakras can help achieve physical, emotional, and spiritual well-being. This weekly meditation plan will introduce you to the essentials of mindfulness meditation. Combined with all the techniques discussed in this book, you can craft a plan that suits you and your lifestyle.

Remember, consistency is key. Whatever plan you design, stick with it and give it time. Surely, you will see the positive impacts it has on you physically, mentally, and spiritually.